pops!

sweets on
a stick!™

Create a Smile with Pops!

Give a kid his own decorated pop, and you'll get back a smile. Somehow, a treat is even sweeter when you can hold it on a stick! That's why pops are the perfect treat to serve at your next party. Everyone gets to grab their own decorated dessert and join in the fun.

In this book, you'll see how these little sweets on a stick create big excitement wherever they go. Just look at the snapshots on our cover for a sample of the amazing shapes you can create. With pops, you can hold a gumball machine, a sailboat, a dinosaur or even a decorated birthday cake in the palm of your hand. And because these treats are made to be displayed standing up, you can arrange a sensational party centerpiece in our Pops Display Stand that everyone will be talking about. Imagine the thrill kids will get when they're greeted by a tower of princess-shaped treats or a basket of colorful balloons that seem to float in mid-air!

It only happens with pops, and this book will show you how easy they are for anyone to do. It all starts with our Favorite Cake Pops Recipe, a tasty mixture of crumbled cake and icing that is easy to shape with your hands or in one of our fun shaped pans and secure on a stick. Give it a dip in Candy Melts and start the decorating fun. The possibilities are endless, as you'll see in the Pops Parade section. We've designed a gallery of more than 100 treats arranged in 6 exciting decorating styles—including fun flowers, tasty toppings, people shaped in our Silicone Boy Mold and elegant treats perfect for sweet tables at any big event.

The gallery is just the beginning of the terrific ideas inside to make your next celebration special! Our 3 celebration sections are packed with exciting treat ideas for every event on your calendar, from birthday parties to holiday gatherings. And because sweets on a stick make perfect gifts, we've also included distinctive ideas for presenting them. Look for our Pops Flower Pot Kit for a fun new way to create an unforgettable homemade treat gift.

It's time to explore the power of pops. Enjoy browsing through all the surprises inside, and start planning your next party with pops!

Marvin Oakes

Marvin Oakes
President
Wilton Enterprises

CREDITS

CREATIVE DIRECTOR
Daniel Masini

SENIOR ART DIRECTOR/POPS DESIGNER
Steve Rocco

ADDITIONAL POPS DESIGN
Mary Gavenda • Jenny Jurewicz • Kathy Krupa
Mark Malak • Amber Spiegel

DECORATING ROOM SUPERVISOR
Cheryl Brown

SENIOR DECORATORS
Mary Gavenda
Susan Matusiak

DECORATORS
Jenny Jurewicz • Diane Knowlton • Kathy Krupa
Mark Malak • Andrea Nickels • Sarah Pistilli
Michele Poto • Valerie Pradhan • Amber Spiegel

RECIPE DEVELOPMENT
Gretchen Homan • Nancy Siler • Beth Somers

EDITOR/WRITER
Jeff Shankman

WRITERS
Mary Enochs • Jane Mikis • Marita Seiler

PRODUCTION MANAGER
Challis Yeager

GRAPHIC DESIGN/PRODUCTION
Courtney Kieras

PHOTOGRAPHY
Black Box Studios
Dale DeBolt
Peter Rossi - PDR Productions

PHOTO STYLIST
Carey Thornton

CREATIVE SERVICES ASSISTANT
Judi Graf

PRODUCT DEVELOPMENT/PUBLICATIONS
Tina Celeste

IN USA
Wilton Industries, Inc.
2240 West 75th Street, Woodridge, IL 60517
www.wilton.com

RETAIL CUSTOMER ORDERS:
Phone: 800.794.5866 • Fax: 888.824.9520

CLASS LOCATIONS:
Phone: 800.942.8881
Online: www.wilton.com/classes

IN CANADA
Wilton Industries Canada Co.
98 Carrier Drive
Etobicoke, Ontario M9W5R1 Canada

RETAIL CUSTOMER ORDERS:
Phone: 416.679.0790

CLASS LOCATIONS:
Phone: 416.679.0790, ext. 200
E-mail: classprograms@wilton.ca

(34)

contents

(76)

(98)

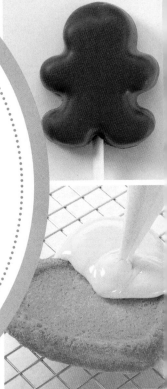

pops basics

Get ready for the most stick-tacular treats that ever popped up at a party! It's time for pops—grabbable goodies on a stick you'll love to dip, decorate and devour. With pops, traditional favorites like cake, cookies, brownies and cereal treats break away from the plate and stand up to join the celebration. Eyes will pop and jaws will drop when your guests see the sensational designs on display (starting on page 14). But first, we need to cover the basic principles of pop-making. Follow our step-by-step instructions and you'll be making professional pops in no time. Stick with us—you're going to have some fun!

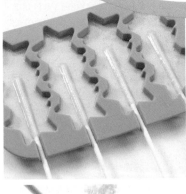

Wilt

what is a pop?

If you can stick it on a stick—it's a pop! Your favorite sweet treats are more fun to eat when you can just grab them and enjoy. The fun factor really goes off the charts when you decorate them with colorful candy and sprinkles! Here's just a sample of the treats you can transform into pops. For more, check out our pops designs starting on page 14.

classic cake pop

Say no to forks and yes to a party cake that each guest can call his own, individually decorated with terrific toppings. Mix the cake and icing together, shape it into a ball and pop it on a stick. See the recipe on page 7.

molded cake pop

Basic Cake Pops can take on many shapes. Pack the mixture into one of Wilton's fun shaped silicone molds and release. Or, fill a dowel rod and push out a tasty tube to make candles, fireworks and more, with fondant and candy trims.

baked cake pop

With Wilton Silicone Cake Pops Molds, you can fill the cavities with your favorite cake mix batter, add a stick and bake a multi-shaped treat, ready to decorate!

brownie pop

The world's favorite chocolatey choice was destined for pop stardom! Don't try this in your favorite square brownie pan—bake individual treats in Wilton Silicone Brownie Molds for the perfect stick-able shapes.

cookie pop

Make your homemade cookies into cookie pops! Cut and bake your favorite shapes using our Roll-Out Cookies recipe and Wilton cutters, then attach a stick with candy. Or, use Wilton shaped cookie pans with sticks and our Vanilla Sugar Cookies on a Stick recipe. Add colorful accents with icing or candy!

cut cake pop

Give the party cake a makeover—use Wilton cutters to create cool theme shapes such as blossoms, people or pets. From there, it's a breeze to give pops personality with icing, fondant or candy.

rice cereal treat pop

Great-tasting cereal treats have never looked this good! Press the mixture into molds or shaped cutters, add a stick and lavish them with tasty trims. It's the ideal party favor or holiday handout!

pops baking essentials

With only a few kitchen basics, you'll have all you need to bake up a batch of pops. Find the designs you want to make starting on page 14, and check the pans we recommend for making them. Next, gather the musts for measuring, mixing and cooling. And don't forget the sticks! See a selection of Wilton baking and decorating products for pops on pages 104-111.

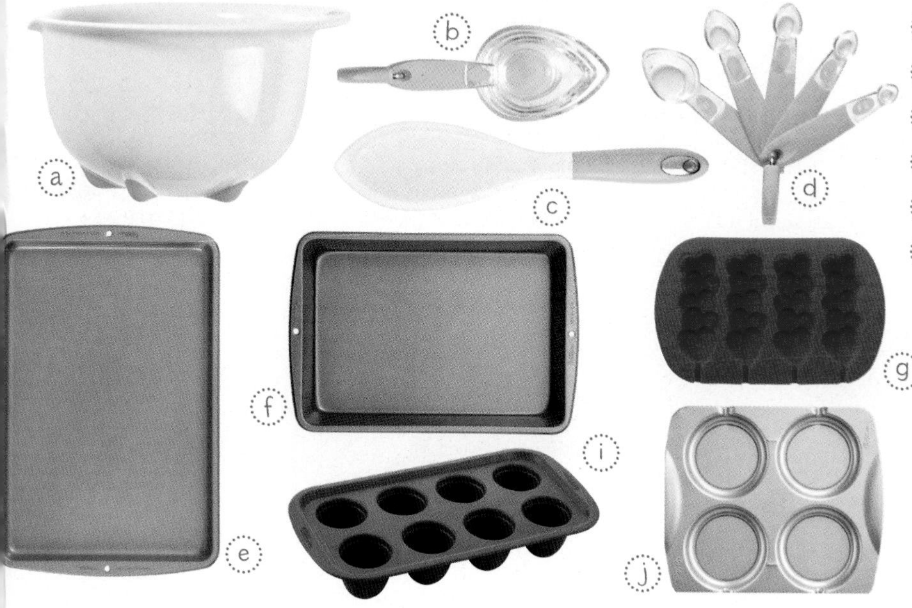

- a Mixing Bowl
- b Measuring Cups
- c Spatula
- d Measuring Spoons
- e 10.5 x 15.5 x 1 in. Jelly Roll Pan
- f 9 x 13 x 2 in. Sheet Pan
- g Silicone Pops Mold
- h Parchment Paper
- i Brownie Pops Pan
- j Cookie Pops Pan
- k 6 in. Cookie Treat Sticks
- l Cooling Grid

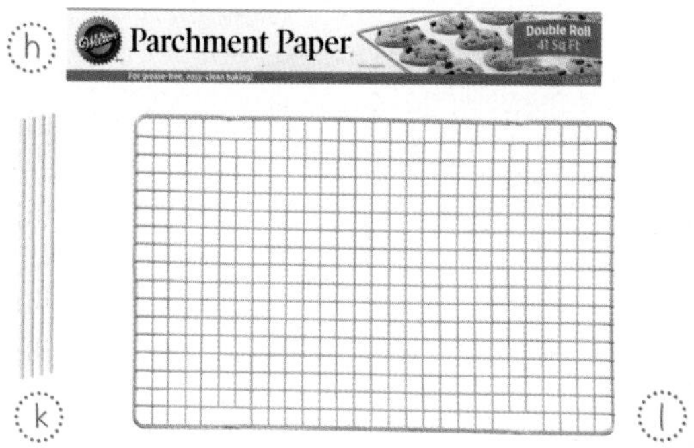

recipes

favorite cake ball pops

box (about 18 oz.) cake mix (your favorite flavor) prepared according to the pound cake recipe below, baked, cooled and halved (freeze the other half for next time)

½ cup creamy icing (your favorite flavor)

bag (14 oz.) Candy Melts, melted following package directions

n large bowl, use hands to crumble cake until no large chunks remain. Add icing and mix with fingers until well combined. Form mixture into cake balls or press into silicone molds (see page 8 for cake ball sizes used in this book). Chill in refrigerator at least 2 hours. f using a silicone mold, carefully remove cake ball shapes. Dip sticks into melted Candy Melts and insert into cake balls; let set. Wait until candy is completely firm before dipping the pops completely in melted Candy Melts; let set. Yields 48 tablespoons.

pound cake from a cake mix

package (18 oz.) cake mix

package (4-serving size) instant pudding and pie filling mix

eggs

cup water

⅓ cup vegetable oil

Preheat oven to 350°F. Spray one 13 x 9 x 2 in. pan or two 8 or 9 x 2 in. round pans with vegetable pan spray.

n large bowl, combine cake mix, pudding mix, eggs, water and oil; beat at medium speed with electric mixer for 2 minutes. Pour into prepared pan. Bake 30-35 minutes for round pans; 35-40 minutes for sheet pan. Cool in pans 10 minutes; remove from pans to cooling grid and cool completely.

mix-ins

Add punch to your pops by blending some of the goodies below into the mix!

Add ½ cup: mini candy-coated chocolates, white chocolate, mini chocolate or butterscotch chips, crushed chocolate or peanut butter sandwich cookies, crushed vanilla wafers or amaretto cookies, chopped peanuts or other favorite nuts, chopped apples or pears, raisins or dried cranberries.

Add 1 tablespoon orange or lemon zest; ⅓ cup mini cinnamon dots; ¼ cup Rainbow Jimmies or other Sprinkles. Or, substitute 4 tablespoons of your favorite jam for 4 tablespoons of icing when mixing.

roll-out cookies

1 cup (2 sticks) unsalted butter, softened

1½ cups granulated sugar

1 egg

1½ teaspoons Pure Vanilla Extract

½ teaspoon Imitation Clear Almond Extract

2¾ cups all-purpose flour

1 teaspoon baking powder

1 teaspoon salt

Preheat oven to 400°F. In large bowl, beat butter and sugar with electric mixer until light and fluffy. Add egg and extracts; mix well. Combine flour, baking powder and salt; add to butter mixture 1 cup at a time, mixing after each addition. Do not chill dough. Divide dough into 2 balls. On a floured surface, roll each ball into a circle approximately 12 in. wide and ⅛ in. thick. Dip cookie cutter in flour before each use. Bake cookies on ungreased cookie sheet 6-7 minutes or until cookies are lightly browned. Makes about 3 dozen cookies. Recipe may be doubled.

vanilla sugar cookies on a stick

(recommended for Wilton Pops Cookie Pans)

1 cup (2 sticks) unsalted butter, softened

1½ cups granulated sugar

1 egg

1½ teaspoons Pure Vanilla Extract

½ teaspoon Imitation Clear Almond Extract

2¾ cups all-purpose flour

2 teaspoons baking powder

1 teaspoon salt

Preheat oven to 350°F. Spray pan with vegetable pan spray. In large bowl, beat butter with sugar until light and fluffy. Add egg and extracts. Combine flour, baking powder and salt; add to butter mixture 1 cup at a time, mixing after each addition. Do not chill dough. Fill cavities with cookie dough to ⅛ in. below top edge; insert sticks into dough, covering 2 in. of end. Bake 20-22 minutes or until cookies are lightly browned. Makes about 12 cookies.

buttercream icing

½ cup solid vegetable shortening

½ cup (1 stick) butter or margarine, softened

1 teaspoon Imitation Clear Vanilla Extract

4 cups sifted confectioners' sugar (about 1 lb.)

2 tablespoons milk

In large bowl, cream shortening and butter with electric mixer. Add vanilla. Gradually add sugar, one cup at a time, beating well on medium speed. Scrape sides and bottom of bowl often. When all sugar has been mixed in, icing will appear dry. Add milk and beat at medium speed until light and fluffy. Keep bowl covered with a damp cloth until ready to use. For best results, keep icing bowl in refrigerator when not in use. Refrigerated in an airtight container, this icing can be stored 2 weeks. Rewhip before using. Makes about 3 cups. For thin (spreading consistency) icing, add 2 tablespoons light corn syrup, water or milk.

color flow icing

(full-strength for outlining)

¼ cup + 1 teaspoon water

4 cups sifted confectioners' sugar (about 1 lb.)

2 tablespoons Color Flow Mix

With electric mixer, using grease-free utensils, blend all ingredients on low speed for 5 minutes. If using hand mixer, use high speed. Color Flow Icing crusts quickly, so keep bowl covered with a damp cloth while using. Stir in desired icing color. Makes about 2 cups.

Thinned Color Flow: To fill in an outlined area, the recipe above must be thinned with ½ teaspoon of water per ¼ cup of icing (just a few drops at a time as you near proper consistency). Use a grease-free spoon or spatula to stir slowly. Color Flow is ready for filling in outlines when a small amount dropped into the mixture takes a count of ten to disappear.

royal icing

3 tablespoons Meringue Powder

4 cups sifted confectioners' sugar (about 1 lb.)

6 tablespoons water*

Beat all ingredients at low speed for 7-10 minutes (10-12 minutes at high speed for portable mixer) until icing forms peaks. Makes about 3 cups.

*When using large countertop mixer or for stiffer icing, use 1 tablespoon less water.

how to mix a cake ball pop

If you've ever rolled meatballs or snowballs, you're ready to make cake balls! Our mixture of crumbled cake and creamy icing holds together to create a perfect round shape. Just bake your cake and let the fun begin (it's also a great way to use cake scraps from other cakes you've baked for the party). Have ½ cup of creamy icing ready, along with a mixing bowl, spatula, measuring cup and baking pan.

1. Cut cake made in a 9 x 13 x 2 in. Sheet Pan in half. In large mixing bowl, use hands to crumble the cake half until no large chunks remain.

2. Add ½ cup of creamy icing. Wilton Creamy Decorator Icing works well along with most brands of ready-to-use icing.

3. Blend in icing completely with a spatula until it is completely combined and holds together cake crumbs.

4. Fill measuring spoon following suggested amounts below. You may need to fill more than once, depending on desired size.

5. Roll back and forth in hands until you create a smooth round ball.

6. Place cake balls on a cookie sheet or baking pan lined with Parchment Paper. Chill for at least 2 hours before inserting sticks following recipe directions.

pop sizes

Making uniform cake ball sizes will really help when you decorate the pops in this book. All project instructions include the recommended pop size, which is easy to achieve when you use a measuring spoon to attain perfect portions.

SMALL
1 tablespoon makes a 1¼ in. diameter ball. One recipe makes 48 small cake balls.

MEDIUM
2 tablespoons make a 1½ in. diameter ball. One recipe makes 24 medium cake balls.

LARGE
3 tablespoons make a 1¾ in. diameter b... One recipe makes 16 large cake balls.

making pops in surprising shapes

A decorated pop is always an unexpected treat—especially when it arrives in shapes folks have never seen before! From cutting and molding to baking in Wilton shaped pans, here's proof that your pop options are up for grabs.

molding in a plasic dowel rod

Wilton dowel rods are the ideal size for molding your pops mixture into a stick-ready cylinder. Great for fireworks, candles, crayons and more.

1. Firmly pack a 3 in. or 4 in. dowel rod completely with cake pops mixture. Insert a Cookie Treat or Loillipop Stick in bottom of dowel rod. Follow project directions on length of stick to leave extended. Chill 2 hours or more.

2. Holding stick, push pop out from top end.

3. Cover with melted candy following project directions.

cutting out shapes

With all the great shapes of Wilton Cookie Cutters, you can make a variety of designs to create an impressive presentation of party pops! Bake your favorite pound cake mix or recipe in the 9 x 13 x 2 in. Sheet Pan or 10.5 x 15.5 x 1 in. Jelly Roll Pan for the ideal consistency that will stay on the stick.

1. Position cutter on cake and push down to meet pan. Remove shape with spatula. Depending on cake depth, you may need to imprint the shape on cake top and cut out shape with a knife.

2. Dip sticks into melted Candy Melts and insert; let set.

3. Dip or cover with candy following project directions.

baking in a silicone mold with a stick

For pops that are 5 times the fun, bake your treats in Wilton multi-shape silicone pops molds. No need to chill after baking—we've included a space that lets you bake with the stick in place.

1. Place mold on cookie sheet. Fill cavities with ⅔ cup of your favorite cake batter. Position stick and turn to coat in batter. Bake following recipe directions; cool on cooling grid.

2. To remove pop, invert mold and apply gentle pressure to the bottom while gently peeling the pan away.

3. Decorate pop with icing or melted candy following project directions. For designs with multiple colors of candy or sprinkles, decorate same-color areas and let set before starting another color.

molding cookie pops

The convenience of baking your treat on the stick makes Wilton Cookie Pops Pans the perfect choice. Be sure to use the Vanilla Sugar Cookies on a Stick recipe (p. 7), which yields the ideal texture of dough that will be secure on the stick.

1. Spray pan cavities with vegetable pan spray. Fill cavities with cookie dough to ⅛ in. below top edge. Insert sticks into dough, covering 2 in. of end or up to stick line shown on pan.

2. Bake following recipe directions. Cool 5 minutes. Gently loosen with spatula; remove from pan. Turn over to release cookies. Cool completely before decorating.

3. Decorate with melted candy or icing following project directions.

baking brownie pops

Flat squares are not the best pick to go on a stick. That's why our Round Brownie Pops Mold is perfect! The dome shape works great and it's ideal for dipping or pouring candy.

1. Spray cavities with vegetable pan spray. Place mold on a cookie sheet. Fill cavities ⅔ full with brownie batter using your favorite mix or recipe. Stick may be inserted before or after baking (secure with melted candy if inserted after

baking). Bake following recipe directions; cool on cooling grid.

2. To remove brownies, apply gentle pressure to bottom while gently peeling the mold away, and lift brownie pop out by stick (if inserted before).

3. Decorate with melted candy or icing following project directions.

molding cake pops in silicone pans

Because our cake ball pops mixture is designed to hold securely to a stick, it will also hold a well-defined shape when pressed into a Wilton silicone mold. You'll find many fun bite-size, petite and mini shapes to choose from for holidays and every day.

1. Firmly pack cavities with cake ball pops mixture. Chill at least 2 hours.

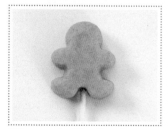

2. To remove treats, apply gentle pressure to bottom while gently peeling the mold away. Insert stick in bottom following pops recipe directions.

3. Decorate with melted candy or icing following project directions.

pops decorating essentials

To make your treats really pop, you need to top them with color and fun! That means having the tools and trims that make the job easy. Below is a sample of the great Wilton products you should have nearby. Be sure to have a variety of colors on hand for decorating diversity! Check pages 104-111 for a complete selection of pops products.

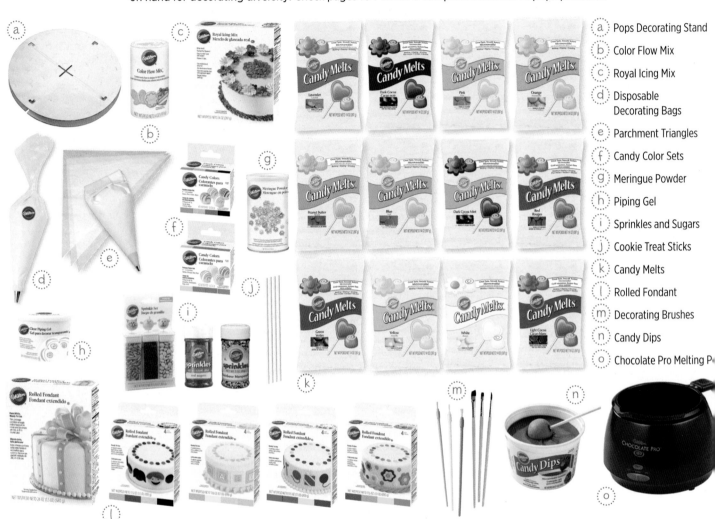

a. Pops Decorating Stand
b. Color Flow Mix
c. Royal Icing Mix
d. Disposable Decorating Bags
e. Parchment Triangles
f. Candy Color Sets
g. Meringue Powder
h. Piping Gel
i. Sprinkles and Sugars
j. Cookie Treat Sticks
k. Candy Melts
l. Rolled Fondant
m. Decorating Brushes
n. Candy Dips
o. Chocolate Pro Melting Pot

pops basics

All our pops designs are different, but most share a few elementary techniques. Before you start decorating, get to know these common pops practices.

inserting a stick

To keep your pop stuck on the stick, follow these easy steps. Having a secure pop helps make decorating (and eating) frustration-free!

1. Dip the end of your Cookie Treat or Lollipop Stick in Candy Melts melted in the Chocolate Pro Melting Pot, or in Candy Dips.

2. Insert stick in chilled pop.

3. Place pops on a parchment-cov[ered] cookie pan or sheet. Chill at leas[t] hours until set.

dipping

Give your pops a dunk in Wilton Candy Melts! Dipping is a great way to seal in the flavor and moistness of the cake and creates a great surface for toppings and decorations. Melt them in the Chocolate Pro Melting Pot, which can handle any size pop in this book. For small and medium cake ball pops, try convenient, microwaveable Wilton Candy Dips.

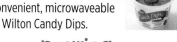

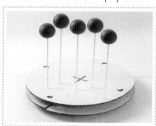

1. Holding the stick securely, dip pop into melted Candy Melts or Candy Dips.

2. Tap pop lightly to smooth surface.

3. Place pops in Pops Decorating Stand. Chill for 10-15 minutes.

pouring

Another easy way to give your pops a smooth surface for decorating—pour on melted candy or thinned icing. Place pops on a cooling grid over a parchment-covered pan to catch the excess icing or candy, which can be reused for additional pops.

1. For cookies, it's optional to seal the back of your pop by icing with melted candy or full-strength icing (see page 12), If you do ice the back, let dry before pouring.

2. Place pop on cooling grid over a parchment-covered cookie sheet. Cover with candy or icing using a cut decorating bag.

3. Let dry completely before decorating.

covering with sprinkles

For quick party pops, after you dip in candy, do a second dip in Wilton Sprinkles! Whether you use nonpareils, jimmies or colored sugars, you'll have an instant colorful treat everyone will love.

1. Dip pop in Candy Melts, then dip in favorite Sprinkles or Sugars.

2. Roll pop until completely covered.

3. Place in Pops Decorating Stand. Chill until firm.

pops techniques

Time to give your pops the finishing touches that make them unforgettable! In a few easy steps, you'll create fun special effects using icing, candy, fondant and Sprinkles. Even if it's your first time decorating, you'll be amazed how great your treats will look!

placing trims with tweezers

For small Sprinkles or shaped Icing Decorations, tweezers are the best tool for precise placement. To attach, pipe a small dot of icing or candy on pop before placing trim.

For a layered look, attach your first layer of Sprinkles with icing or candy. Let set, then begin the next layer.

Be sure to position the tweezers properly to avoid knocking off other decorations. Hold trims in place for a few seconds to be sure they are secure.

Keep a few types of tweezers on hand. For tight spaces, using angled tweezers makes applying Sprinkles more convenient.

applying sugar to fondant

A dusting of sugar adds dazzle to your fondant accents, boosting the dimension and color.

1. Brush fondant trims with a small amount of water or Piping Gel.

2. Hold pop over a bowl and sprinkle with Wilton Colored Sugar, Sparkling Sugar or Cake Sparkles.

3. Let set upright or insert in the Pops Decorating Stand.

piping cornelli lace

Proof that pops can travel in sophisticated circles. This technique features a continuous curving line which never overlaps or touches, giving it a light, lacy look. If you plan to serve pops as part of your shower sweet table, there couldn't be a better choice.

1. Use tip 1, 2 or cut parchment bag and melted candy or icing. Hold the bag close to the pop so that line attaches without scraping pop with tip. Pipe a continuous line, curving it up, down and around.

2. Pipe until the entire pop is covered. Make sure line never touches or crosses and don't leave any loose ends.

3. Stop pressure, pull bag away. Chill until firm.

marbleizing

Luxurious swirled colors of Wilton Candy Melts add fascinating flair to the simple dipped pop. Generally, pairing a light and dark color works best, but try your own fun color combinations to suit the occasion!

1. Separately melt 2 different colors of Candy Melts. Stir colors together, using a lollipop stick to draw lines in mixture. Do not overmix. Dip pop into mixture.

2. Turn pop in mixture to marbleize. Tap pop on side of bowl or Melting Pot to smooth surface.

3. Place pop in Pops Decorating Stand. Chill until firm.

icing & pouring

For cake pops, it is especially important to seal the entire surface to prevent drying out. If you are pouring candy or thinned icing, only the top side will be covered—therefore, you need to ice the bottom with melted candy or icing before you pour.

1. Use a spatula to ice bottom of treat smooth with melted candy or thinned icing. Chill until firm.

2. Place treat on a cooling grid above a parchment-covered cookie sheet or baking pan. Pipe or pour melted candy or icing over treat. Excess candy will drip down to pan to be used for more pops.

3. Place treat, bottom side down, on parchment paper and chill until firm.

tri-dipping

Create a rainbow effect with 3 layers of color on 1 pop! Works with any trio of Candy Melts colors, or try light, medium and dark shades of the same color. You can lighten any Candy Melts color by adding melted white Candy Melts.

1. Start with a pop that has already been dipped and chilled as your base color. Dip pop ⅔ deep in your second color of melted Candy Melts. Be sure to dip

straight down to create an even line between colors. Tap and chill.

2. Dip pop ⅓ deep in third Candy Melts color. Tap to remove excess.

3. Place pop on parchment-covered board and chill until firm.

brush embroidery

Give pops a soft, dappled texture by lightly brushing your icing border toward the center of the pop. This technique works best using the square tip brush from the Wilton Brush Set.

1. Thin royal or buttercream icing with Piping Gel. Pipe a section or two of border using the tip and technique specified in project instructions. Before icing can dry, brush lines of icing toward center of design with damp brush.

2. Work in quick, short strokes. Clean brush with water frequently to create distinct lines of icing. Repeat technique for inner borders.

3. Lay flat to dry or place in Pops Decorating Stand following project directions.

candy grass

A scenic way to present your pop—serve it on a bed of candy grass made in a Wilton Baking Cup. Makes an ideal base for jungle or floral themed brownie pops.

1. Pipe a layer of melted Candy Melts in the bottom of a standard Wilton Baking Cup.

2. Pipe tapering lines of melted candy up the side of the cup, creating a grass effect. Chill until firm.

3. Peel off baking cup and position pop when needed.

curlicues

Fondant frills make any pop more lively! Use curlicues for hair and curling ribbons on gift pops.

1. Roll out fondant ⅛ in. thick on Roll & Cut Mat lightly dusted with cornstarch. Cut into thin strips.

2. Loosely wrap strips around a Lollipop or Cookie Treat Stick several times. Let set for 5 to 10 minutes.

3. Slide curl off stick and let dry. Attach to treat with candy or icing.

bows

Wrap up a pops package with an easy bow made with thin strips of fondant. Adding fondant accents such as bows is a quick way to give a flat pop dimension and color.

1. Roll out fondant ¹⁄₁₆ in. thick on Roll & Cut Mat lightly dusted with cornstarch. Cut into ¼ in. or ⅛ in. wide strips following project directions.

2. Cut a long and a short length strip for each pop, following project directions. Brush ends of strips with water. Fold ends toward center and press lightly to attach.

3. Roll a small fondant ball for knot; flatten. Attach bows and knot with damp brush.

palm tree

Wait until the kids see your jungle pops display with a giant palm tree at the top of our Pops Display Stand! When the tree is assembled, insert it in a base of fondant-covered cereal treats.

1. Add ½ teaspoon Gum-Tex to 4 oz. Rolled Fondant tinted Leaf Green. Roll out ⅛ in. thick on Roll & Cut Mat lightly dusted with cornstarch. Cut 8 leaves using largest Leaf Cut-Out (make extras to allow for breakage). Cut notches using a knife.

2. Let leaves dry overnight on cornstarch-dusted Wave Flower Former.

3. Roll a 1 in. ball of green fondant for base. Make indent in bottom for pretzel rod. Place in small Flower Forming Cup. Grouping in 2 layers of 3 and a top layer of 2, insert ends of leaves in ball and

remove. Pipe melted candy in openings and reinsert leaves. Pipe additional candy between leaves. Chill until firm. Insert pretzel rod in base and attach treetop and fondant coconuts following project instructions.

blossom

Use Wilton Cut-Outs like cookie cutters to make fondant flowers that really dress up pops. Create a bouquet of assorted colors using our Fondant Multi Packs.

1. Roll out fondant ⅛ in. thick on Roll & Cut Mat lightly dusted with cornstarch. Cut blossoms using small Flower Cut-Outs.

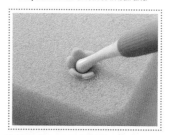

2. Place flowers on thick Fondant Shaping Foam. Cup center by pressing with small end of Dogbone Tool.

3. Attach a White Sugar Pearl for center with a dot of icing, Piping Gel or melted candy.

pops parade

You never have to make the same pop twice! In this section, we'll show you the plethora of ideas you can make starting with one great theme—from fun faces and flowers to tempting toppings and special occasion designs.

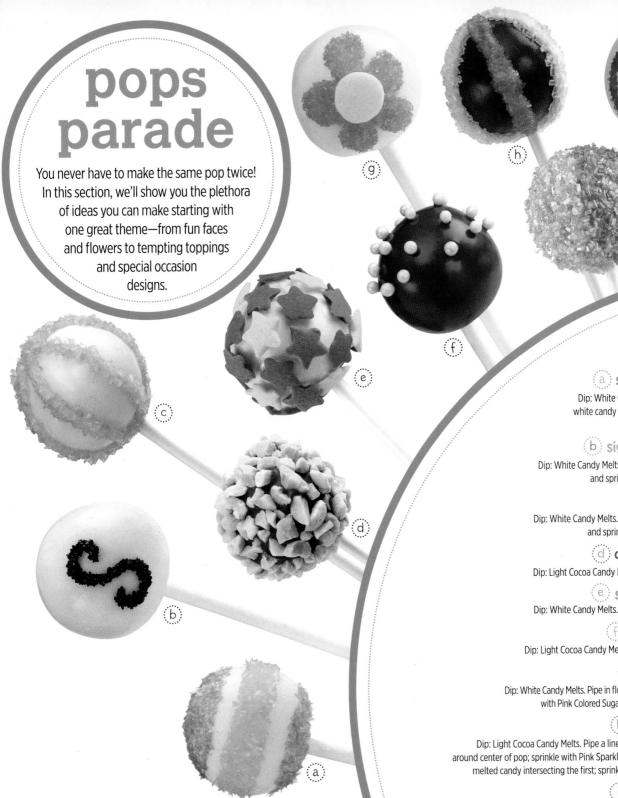

a sparkling stripes
Dip: White Candy Melts. Pipe stripes with white candy and sprinkle with Pink, Yellow and Orange Cake Sparkles.

b signature sprinkle
Dip: White Candy Melts. Pipe letter with white candy and sprinkle with Black Colored Sugar.

c baby blue
Dip: White Candy Melts. Pipe stripes with white candy and sprinkle with Blue Sparkling Sugar.

d chopped up pop
Dip: Light Cocoa Candy Melts. Dip in chopped peanuts.

e star spectacular
Dip: White Candy Melts. Attach Jumbo Stars Sprinkles.

f pearl treasure
Dip: Light Cocoa Candy Melts. Attach White Sugar Pearls.

g daisy dazzler
Dip: White Candy Melts. Pipe in flower with white candy; sprinkle with Pink Colored Sugar. Attach Jumbo Confetti center.

h sprinkled pink
Dip: Light Cocoa Candy Melts. Pipe a line of melted White Candy Melts around center of pop; sprinkle with Pink Sparkling Sugar. Pipe another line of melted candy intersecting the first; sprinkle with White Sparkling Sugar.

i striking it rich
Dip: White Candy Melts. Dip half in Silver, half in Gold Pearlized Sugars.

j scarlet spiral
Dip: White Candy Melts. Pipe swirl with melted white candy Sprinkle with Red Colored Sugar

k bounty of blossoms
Dip: White Candy Melts. Attach Jumbo Daisies Sprinkles; pipe centers with melted white candy

terrific toppings!

Pop principle #1: make them delicious! Here's how we roll—in sugars, nuts, sprinkles and all kinds of tasty and tasteful toppings that will have your guests coming back for more. Make your Favorite Cake Ball Pops using cake baked in a 9 x 13 x 2 in. Sheet Pan, roll them in any size, dip them in White or Light Cocoa Candy Melts, chill for 1-2 minutes and add your favorite appetizing accents. Candy is piped using a cut parchment bag.

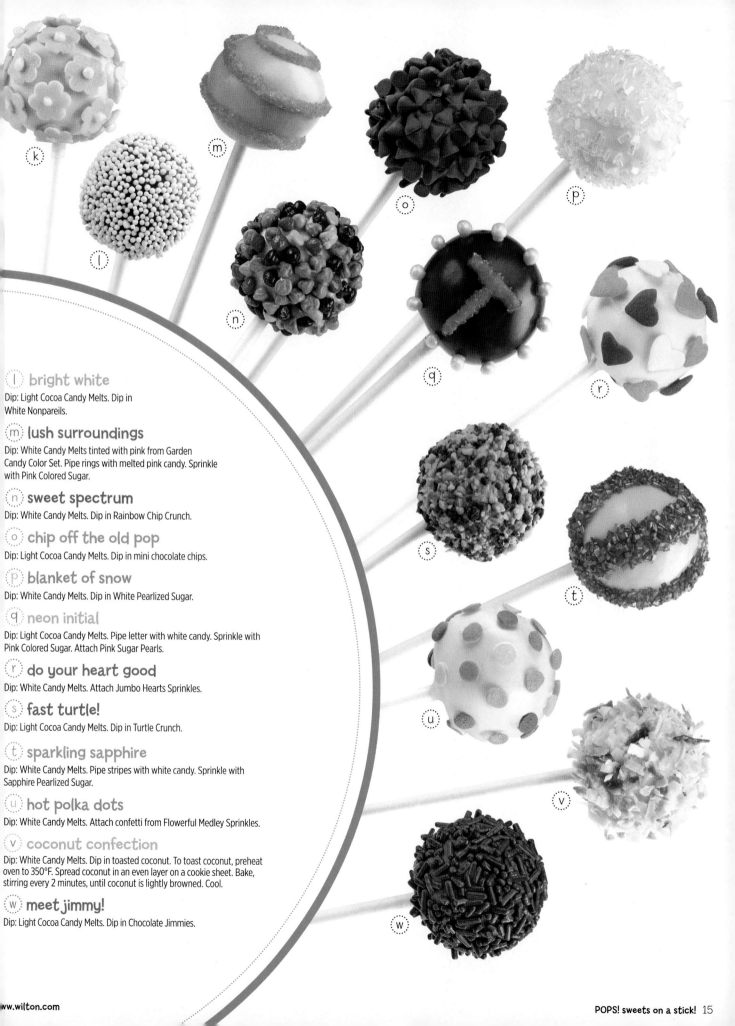

l) bright white
Dip: Light Cocoa Candy Melts. Dip in White Nonpareils.

m) lush surroundings
Dip: White Candy Melts tinted with pink from Garden Candy Color Set. Pipe rings with melted pink candy. Sprinkle with Pink Colored Sugar.

n) sweet spectrum
Dip: White Candy Melts. Dip in Rainbow Chip Crunch.

o) chip off the old pop
Dip: Light Cocoa Candy Melts. Dip in mini chocolate chips.

p) blanket of snow
Dip: White Candy Melts. Dip in White Pearlized Sugar.

q) neon initial
Dip: Light Cocoa Candy Melts. Pipe letter with white candy. Sprinkle with Pink Colored Sugar. Attach Pink Sugar Pearls.

r) do your heart good
Dip: White Candy Melts. Attach Jumbo Hearts Sprinkles.

s) fast turtle!
Dip: Light Cocoa Candy Melts. Dip in Turtle Crunch.

t) sparkling sapphire
Dip: White Candy Melts. Pipe stripes with white candy. Sprinkle with Sapphire Pearlized Sugar.

u) hot polka dots
Dip: White Candy Melts. Attach confetti from Flowerful Medley Sprinkles.

v) coconut confection
Dip: White Candy Melts. Dip in toasted coconut. To toast coconut, preheat oven to 350°F. Spread coconut in an even layer on a cookie sheet. Bake, stirring every 2 minutes, until coconut is lightly browned. Cool.

w) meet jimmy!
Dip: Light Cocoa Candy Melts. Dip in Chocolate Jimmies.

have a brownie blast!

Your favorite fudgy treats are now more fun than you can shake a stick at! Just bake them in the Silicone Round Brownie Pops Mold, insert a stick and start decorating with your favorite colorful candy and sprinkles. All designs are dipped in Candy Melts, then chilled until firm and decorated as stated at right; candy is piped using a cut parchment bag. For an alternative to chocolate, use the Pound Cake from a Cake Mix recipe (p. 7)—it comes out great in the Brownie Pops Mold.

a frosty foliage
Dip: Light Cocoa Candy Melts. Pipe leaves with melted White Candy Melts, finish with brush embroidery technique. Pipe dots with melted White Candy Melts

b sun and sea shades
Dip: Yellow Candy Melts. Pipe zigzags with melted Blue Candy Melts. Attach confetti from Flowerful Medley Sprinkles with melted Yellow Candy Melts

c linked in love
Dip: Red Candy Melts. Attach Jumbo Hearts Sprinkles with melted cand

d sundae makes your day
Dip: White Candy Melts. Pipe chocolate drips with melted Light Cocoa Candy Melts Attach Rainbow Jimmies and Cinnamon Drops Sprinkles

e rainbow rows
Dip: Light Cocoa Candy Melts. Pipe zigzags with melted Pink, Green Blue, Yellow and Orange Candy Melts

f frazzled friend
Dip: Orange Candy Melts. Pipe nose with a dot of melted Orange Candy Melts Attach confetti from Flowerful Medley Sprinkles for eyes and ears Jumbo Nonpareils for pupils, Chocolate Jimmies for mouth

g bright birdcage
Dip: White Candy Melts tinted with green from Garden Candy Color Se Pipe lines with melted Orange, Blue and Yellow Candy Melts

h luscious letter
Dip: Light Cocoa Candy Melts. Pipe initial with melted White Candy Melts

i pink & polka dots
Dip: White Candy Melts tinted with pink from Garden Candy Color Set. Attach confett from Flowerful Medley Sprinkles with melted pink candy

j colorful curliques
Dip: Green Candy Melts lightened with White Candy Melts. Pipe loops and bea border with White Candy Melts tinted with pink from Garden Candy Color Se

k nonpareil thril
Dip: Light Cocoa Candy Melts. Pipe swags with melted Light Cocoa Candy Melt Immediately sprinkle with Rainbow Nonpareil

l sunshine bloom
Dip: Yellow Candy Melts. Cut flower from rose-tinted fondan using medium Flower Cut-Out. Roll a ¼ in. violet fondar center; attach to pop with melted candy. Pipe stem an leaf using melted White Candy Melts tinted with gree from Garden Candy Color Se

Wilt

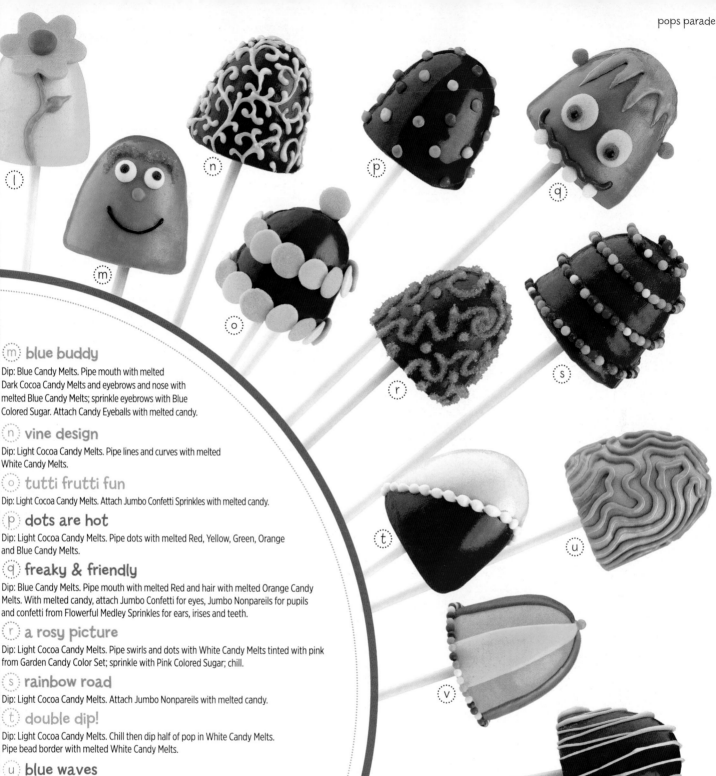

m blue buddy
Dip: Blue Candy Melts. Pipe mouth with melted Dark Cocoa Candy Melts and eyebrows and nose with melted Blue Candy Melts; sprinkle eyebrows with Blue Colored Sugar. Attach Candy Eyeballs with melted candy.

n vine design
Dip: Light Cocoa Candy Melts. Pipe lines and curves with melted White Candy Melts.

o tutti frutti fun
Dip: Light Cocoa Candy Melts. Attach Jumbo Confetti Sprinkles with melted candy.

p dots are hot
Dip: Light Cocoa Candy Melts. Pipe dots with melted Red, Yellow, Green, Orange and Blue Candy Melts.

q freaky & friendly
Dip: Blue Candy Melts. Pipe mouth with melted Red and hair with melted Orange Candy Melts. With melted candy, attach Jumbo Confetti for eyes, Jumbo Nonpareils for pupils and confetti from Flowerful Medley Sprinkles for ears, irises and teeth.

r a rosy picture
Dip: Light Cocoa Candy Melts. Pipe swirls and dots with White Candy Melts tinted with pink from Garden Candy Color Set; sprinkle with Pink Colored Sugar; chill.

s rainbow road
Dip: Light Cocoa Candy Melts. Attach Jumbo Nonpareils with melted candy.

t double dip!
Dip: Light Cocoa Candy Melts. Chill then dip half of pop in White Candy Melts. Pipe bead border with melted White Candy Melts.

u blue waves
Dip: Pink Candy Melts. Pipe swirls with melted Blue Candy Melts.

v treat tones
Dip: Orange Candy Melts. Pipe in sections approximately ½ in. wide with melted Red, Green, Blue and Yellow Candy Melts. Attach Jumbo Rainbow Nonpareils with melted candy.

w simple drizzle
Dip: Light Cocoa Candy Melts. Drizzle pop with melted White Candy Melts.

x a spot of cocoa
Dip: White Candy Melts tinted with pink from Garden Candy Color Set. Pipe dots and bead border with melted Light Cocoa Candy Melts.

The Silicone Round Brownie Pops Mold (2105-4925) gives you a time-saving option. Bake your favorite brownie mix or recipe, unmold and you're ready to decorate a perfectly-shaped treat.

sprinkled personalities!

More than just tasty ways to top your pops, Sprinkles add a new dimension of detail and fun! Decorate all these friendly faces with our most popular Sprinkles, to make cool hairdos, facial features and accessories. Use tweezers to put them in the perfect position and attach with melted candy. All treats are made with the Favorite Cake Ball Pops recipe (p. 7) using cake baked in the 9 x 13 x 2 in. Sheet Pan, and dipped in Candy Melts. Chill until firm and decorate using Sprinkles listed. Candy Melts are piped using a cut parchment bag.

a gone hollywood
Dip: White Candy Melts tinted with a little Light Cocoa Candy Melts. Attach Jumbo Stars for lenses and Rainbow Jimmies for frames. Attach Chocolate Jimmies for hair. Pipe mouth with White Candy Melts tinted with black from Garden Candy Color Set

b check your makeup
Dip: Yellow Candy Melts. Attach People Pops Sprinkles for features. Pipe hair with Red Candy Melts, pupils and eyelashes with White Candy Melts tinted with black from Garden Candy Color Set

c poultry pop
Dip: Orange Candy Melts. Attach Animal Pops Sprinkles for wings, feet, beak and hair. Pipe eyes and beak lines with White Candy Melts tinted with black from Garden Candy Color Set

d space face
Dip: Green Candy Melts. Attach black shoestring licorice for antennae, Jumbo Confetti for tips Candy Eyeballs. Pipe mouth with White Candy Melts tinted with black from Garden Candy Color Set

e girl with curls
Dip: Blue Candy Melts. Attach Jumbo Confetti for hair, Candy Eyeballs, Rainbow Nonpareil for nose and Chocolate Jimmy for mouth

f sleepy creature
Dip: White Candy Melts tinted with pink from Garden Candy Color Set. Attach Animal Sprinkles for ears Pipe eyes and mouth with White Candy Melts tinted with black from Garden Candy Color Set

g lovestruck lass
Dip: White Candy Melts tinted with orange from Primary Candy Color Set. Pipe hair with Yellow Candy Melts, nose with orange-tinted candy and mouth with White Candy Melts tinted with black from Garden Candy Color Set. Attach Jumbo Hearts for bow, Jumbo Nonpareil for knot, Pink Hearts from Flowerful Medley Sprinkles for eyes, White Sugar Pearls for earrings

h mohawk man
Dip: White Candy Melts tinted with orange from Primary Candy Color Set. Attach Chocolate Jimmies for hair and Rainbow Jimmies for mouth. Pipe in glasses; cover with Black Colored Sugar. Pipe nose and ears with orange tinted candy. Attach Jumbo Nonpareil for earring

i curly top
Dip: Orange Candy Melts. Attach Candy Eyeballs and Jumbo Nonpareils for hair Pipe mouth and nose with melted orange candy. Attach confetti from Flowerful Medley Sprinkles for cheeks

j not feeling blue at all!
Dip: Blue Candy Melts. Attach People Pops Sprinkles for eyes and eyebrows. Pipe pupils and nose with melted blue candy, irises and mouth with White Candy Melts tinted with black from Garden Candy Color Set, teeth with melted white candy

k beauty queen
Dip: White Candy Melts tinted with orange from Primary Candy Color Set Pipe hair and features with Yellow Candy Melts, nose with orange tinted candy and eyes and mouth with White Candy Melts tinted with black from Garden Candy Color Set. Attach People Pops Sprinkles for crown and collar

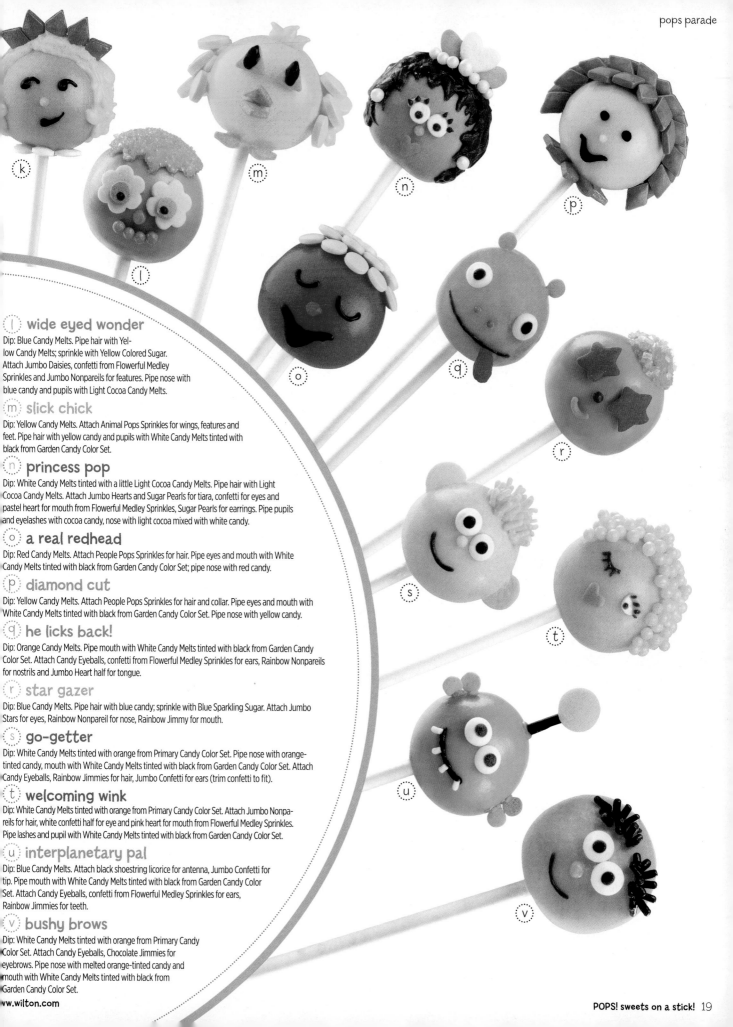

l wide eyed wonder

Dip: Blue Candy Melts. Pipe hair with Yellow Candy Melts; sprinkle with Yellow Colored Sugar. Attach Jumbo Daisies, confetti from Flowerful Medley Sprinkles and Jumbo Nonpareils for features. Pipe nose with blue candy and pupils with Light Cocoa Candy Melts.

m slick chick

Dip: Yellow Candy Melts. Attach Animal Pops Sprinkles for wings, features and feet. Pipe hair with yellow candy and pupils with White Candy Melts tinted with black from Garden Candy Color Set.

n princess pop

Dip: White Candy Melts tinted with a little Light Cocoa Candy Melts. Pipe hair with Light Cocoa Candy Melts. Attach Jumbo Hearts and Sugar Pearls for tiara, confetti for eyes and pastel heart for mouth from Flowerful Medley Sprinkles, Sugar Pearls for earrings. Pipe pupils and eyelashes with cocoa candy, nose with light cocoa mixed with white candy.

o a real redhead

Dip: Red Candy Melts. Attach People Pops Sprinkles for hair. Pipe eyes and mouth with White Candy Melts tinted with black from Garden Candy Color Set; pipe nose with red candy.

p diamond cut

Dip: Yellow Candy Melts. Attach People Pops Sprinkles for hair and collar. Pipe eyes and mouth with White Candy Melts tinted with black from Garden Candy Color Set. Pipe nose with yellow candy.

q he licks back!

Dip: Orange Candy Melts. Pipe mouth with White Candy Melts tinted with black from Garden Candy Color Set. Attach Candy Eyeballs, confetti from Flowerful Medley Sprinkles for ears, Rainbow Nonpareils for nostrils and Jumbo Heart half for tongue.

r star gazer

Dip: Blue Candy Melts. Pipe hair with blue candy; sprinkle with Blue Sparkling Sugar. Attach Jumbo Stars for eyes, Rainbow Nonpareil for nose, Rainbow Jimmy for mouth.

s go-getter

Dip: White Candy Melts tinted with orange from Primary Candy Color Set. Pipe nose with orange-tinted candy, mouth with White Candy Melts tinted with black from Garden Candy Color Set. Attach Candy Eyeballs, Rainbow Jimmies for hair, Jumbo Confetti for ears (trim confetti to fit).

t welcoming wink

Dip: White Candy Melts tinted with orange from Primary Candy Color Set. Attach Jumbo Nonpareils for hair, white confetti half for eye and pink heart for mouth from Flowerful Medley Sprinkles. Pipe lashes and pupil with White Candy Melts tinted with black from Garden Candy Color Set.

u interplanetary pal

Dip: Blue Candy Melts. Attach black shoestring licorice for antenna, Jumbo Confetti for tip. Pipe mouth with White Candy Melts tinted with black from Garden Candy Color Set. Attach Candy Eyeballs, confetti from Flowerful Medley Sprinkles for ears, Rainbow Jimmies for teeth.

v bushy brows

Dip: White Candy Melts tinted with orange from Primary Candy Color Set. Attach Candy Eyeballs, Chocolate Jimmies for eyebrows. Pipe nose with melted orange-tinted candy and mouth with White Candy Melts tinted with black from Garden Candy Color Set.

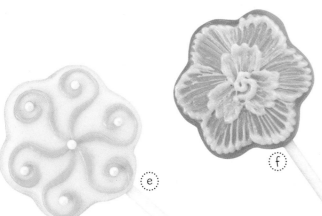

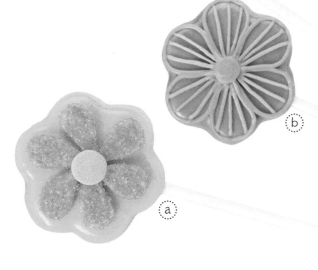

goodies from the garden

Pick some wild flowers from our garden and start the decorating fun! Let Mother Nature try on some crazy new color combos and dazzling designs such as sunbursts, spirals, hearts and more. All flowers are made with the Pound Cake from a Cake Mix recipe (p. 7) baked in our 10.5 x 15.5 x 1 in. Jelly Roll Pan and cut using our large Flower Cut-Out. Designs are dipped in Candy Melts, then chilled until firm and decorated as stated; Candy Melts are piped using a cut parchment bag.

ⓐ **strong shades**
Dip: Yellow Candy Melts. Pipe in petals with melted White Candy Melts tinted with pink from Garden Candy Color Set; sprinkle with Pink Colored Sugar. Attach Jumbo Confetti center with melted Candy Melts

ⓑ **bright stripes**
Dip: Blue Candy Melts. Pipe lines with melted Yellow Candy Melts Outline petals and pipe in center with melted Blue Candy Melts

ⓒ **multi-faceted flower**
Dip: White Candy Melts tinted with pink from Garden Candy Color Set. Outline petals with melted Blue Candy Melts; sprinkle with Blue Colored Sugar. Pipe in inner petals with melted White Candy Melts tinted with violet from Garden Candy Color Set; sprinkle with Lavender Colored Sugar. Attach confetti from Flowerful Medley Sprinkles for center with melted candy

ⓓ **flavorful flower**
Dip: Light Cocoa Candy Melts. Pipe swirls with melted Yellow Candy Melts

ⓔ **pick pink!**
Dip: White Candy Melts. Pipe swirls with White Candy Melts tinted with pink from Garden Candy Color Set. Attach White Sugar Pearls with melted candy

ⓕ **dappled daisy**
Dip: Blue Candy Melts. Outline flower with White Candy Melts; finish with brush embroidery technique; repeat for inner petals and pipe center with melted candy

ⓖ **latticework pop**
Dip: White Candy Melts. Outline petals with Orange Candy Melts. Pipe in center with White Candy Melts tinted with pink from Garden Candy Color Set. Add lines with melted Blue, Pink and Orange candy

ⓗ **center of attention**
Dip: White Candy Melts tinted with pink from Garden Candy Color Set. Attach Jumbo Daisy Sprinkle center and add outlines with Yellow Candy Melts

ⓘ **sparkling stems**
Dip: Blue Candy Melts. Outline flower with melted Lavender Candy Melts; sprinkle with Lavender Colored Sugar. Repeat with Yellow and Blue Candy Melts and Colored Sugar

ⓙ **pinwheel petals**
Dip: Light Cocoa Candy Melts. Pipe curls with White Candy Melts; repeat with Blue Candy Melts. Add beads and center dot with White Candy Melt

ⓚ **wow factor**
Dip: Yellow Candy Melts. After dipping, immediately sprinkle top with Yellow Colored Sugar. Outline petals and pipe dot center with Blue Candy Melt

lots of dots
Dip: Orange Candy Melts. Outline petals and pipe dots with melted Lavender Candy Melts. Attach confetti from Flowerful Medley Sprinkles for center with melted candy.

all heart
Dip: Light Cocoa Candy Melts. Outline hearts on petals with White Candy Melts tinted with pink from Garden Candy Color Set; sprinkle with Pink Colored Sugar. Attach Jumbo Hearts and confetti from Flowerful Medley Sprinkles for center with melted candy.

cool contrasts
Dip: Lavender Candy Melts. Pipe in inner petals with melted Blue Candy Melts. Attach Pink Jumbo Daisy with melted candy.

fancy frills
Dip: Light Cocoa Candy Melts. Outline petals and pipe scrollwork with melted White Candy Melts. Edge petals with beads in White Candy Melts.

glow forth
Dip: Orange Candy Melts. Pipe in petals with melted Blue Candy Melts; immediately outline with melted Yellow Candy Melts. Attach confetti from Flowerful Medley Sprinkles for center.

petal points
Dip: Light Cocoa Candy Melts. Attach confetti from Flowerful Medley Sprinkles for center. Pipe beads with Orange Candy Melts.

blushing blossom
Dip: White Candy Melts tinted with pink from Garden Candy Color Set. Attach White Sugar Pearls with pink candy.

deep purple
Dip: White Candy Melts tinted with violet from Garden Candy Color Set. After dipping sprinkle with Lavender Colored Sugar. Attach Jumbo Confetti. Pipe lines with melted violet candy.

bold in blue
Dip: White Candy Melts. Outline flower with Blue Candy Melts; sprinkle with Blue Colored Sugar. Attach Pink Jumbo Confetti center with melted candy.

natural whirl
Dip: White Candy Melts tinted with pink from Garden Candy Color Set. Pipe spirals with melted Blue Candy Melts. Attach confetti from Flowerful Medley Sprinkles for center with melted candy.

lively and lovely
Dip: Light Cocoa Candy Melts. Outline petals with melted candy; sprinkle with Rainbow Nonpareils. Attach Jumbo Confetti center with melted candy.

Wilton Flower Cut-Outs (417-435) are the ideal sizes for your petaled sweets on a stick. Works great for pound cake or cookies.

a) **fleur de-light**

Dip: Light Cocoa Candy Melts. Pipe beac
fleur-de-lis and dots with White Candy Melts

b) **pink presence**

Dip: Use White Candy Melts tinted with pink from Garder
Candy Color Set; chill, dip half in Light Cocoa Candy Melts. Pipe
dots with melted pink candy

c) **fancy pansy**

Dip: White Candy Melts. Pipe in flower with Blue Candy Melts
add swirl with Yellow Candy Melts

d) **fascinating lace**

Dip: Light Cocoa Candy Melts. Pipe cornelli lace with White Candy Melts

e) **zesty zigzags**

Dip: Light Cocoa Candy Melts. Pipe zigzags with Pink Candy Melts, dots with Yellow Candy Melts

f) **impressive initial**

Dip: White Candy Melts. Pipe letter with Light Cocoa Candy Melts

g) **chevron chic**

Dip: Light Cocoa Candy Melts. Pipe v-shape with Pink and White Candy Melts, starting a
center point and building up a dot at each end

h) **all buttoned up**

Dip: Use White Candy Melts for entire pop; chill, then dip half of pop in Yellow Candy Melts. Pipe
line and dots with Light Cocoa Candy Melts

i) **sweet spot**

Dip: Light Cocoa Candy Melts. Pipe dots with White Candy Melts

j) **whirlwind**

Dip: White Candy Melts. Tint additional white with green from Garder
Candy Color Set. Drizzle around pop

k) **floral fence**

Dip: Pink Candy Melts. Pipe lines with Pink Candy Melts, dot flowers
with White Candy Melts

l) **blue web**

Dip: Light Cocoa Candy Melts. Tint White Candy Melts with blue from
Primary Candy Color Set; drizzle around pop

the height
of elegance!

Here are pops with the poise it takes to make your receptions exceptional!
Featuring refined designs and classic colors, these treats will work for favors or
sweet tables at any occasion. Change the colors to complement your look. Make the
Favorite Cake Ball Pops recipe using cake baked in our 9 x 13 x 2 in. Sheet Pan; roll
balls in any size. All designs are dipped in Candy Melts, then chilled until firm and
decorated as stated at right. Candy Melts are piped using a cut parchment bag.

m star turn
Dip: Light Cocoa Candy Melts. Pipe in stars with White Candy Melts.

n tendril treat
Dip: Light Cocoa Candy Melts. Pipe line and spirals with Yellow Candy Melts.

o winding lines
Dip: Use Light Cocoa Candy Melts for entire pop; chill, then dip half of pop in White Candy Melts. Drizzle lines around pop with Light Cocoa Candy Melts.

p party circuit
Dip: Use White Candy Melts tinted with pink from Garden Candy Color Set for entire pop; chill, then dip half of pop in White Candy Melts. Pipe line and dots with Light Cocoa Candy Melts.

q sublime scrollwork
Dip: Light Cocoa Candy Melts. Pipe scallops and fleurs-de-lis with Light Cocoa Candy Melts.

r refinements
Dip: Use White Candy Melts for entire pop; chill then dip each side of pop in Light Cocoa Candy Melts. Pipe beads with white candy. Attach Pink Sugar Pearls with white candy.

s upbeat beading
Dip: Light Cocoa Candy Melts. Pipe line and beads with White Candy Melts.

t pastel twists
Dip: White Candy Melts. Pipe spirals with White Candy Melts tinted with blue from Primary Candy Color Set.

u sprouting sweetly
Dip: White Candy Melts. Pipe curls and dots with Light Cocoa Candy Melts.

v brushstrokes
Dip: Light Cocoa Candy Melts. Pipe flower with White Candy Melts; finish with brush embroidery technique.

w posh pop
Dip: Use White Candy Melts tinted with pink from Garden Candy Color Set for entire pop; chill, then dip half of pop in Light Cocoa Candy Melts. Pipe fleurs-de-lis with White Candy Melts.

x fudge flow
Dip: White Candy Melts. Pipe drips with Light Cocoa Candy Melts.

populate the party with one great pan!

You can gather quite a crowd when you create pops using the Wilton Silicone Boy Mold! Just press your Favorite Cake Ball Pops mixture (p. 7) into the cavities for your basic profile, spatula bottoms and cover tops with Candy Melts in your choice of skin tone and dress them up with melted candy and Sprinkles. Candy is piped using a cut parchment bag. Make various skin tones using melted White Candy Melts—for lighter shades, add a little orange from Primary Candy Color Set; for darker shades, add melted Light Cocoa Candy Melts to white. We're just scratching the surface here—use your imagination to create your own pops pals!

a screamin' demon
Coating: Orange Candy Melts. Attach Candy Eyeballs. Pipe lines and features with Blue, Orange and White Candy Melts tinted with black from Garden Candy Color Set.

b cow poke
Coating: White Candy Melts tinted with orange from Primary Candy Color Set. Pipe in clothes and details with White, Blue, Red and Light Cocoa Candy Melts. Shape hat and hat band using rolled fondant tinted brown and red.

c majestic miss
Coating: White Candy Melts tinted with orange from Primary Candy Color Set. Cut and shape dress with fondant tinted violet. Pipe violet candy dress details and sprinkle with Lavender Colored Sugar. Pipe hair with Yellow Candy Melts. Attach diamonds from People Pops Sprinkle Set and make wand with White Candy Melts on parchment then attach heart from Flowerful Medley Sprinkles.

d scuba buddy
Coating: White Candy Melts tinted with orange from Primary Candy Color Set. Pipe in trunks with Yellow Candy Melts and hair and features with Light Cocoa Candy Melts. Shape snorkel, mask and flippers with blue tinted fondant.

e cheerful chef
Coating: White Candy Melts tinted with orange from Primary Candy Color Set. Pipe in apron with White Candy Melts and shoes with white candy tinted with black from Garden Candy Color Set. Pipe hair and features with Light Cocoa Candy Melts; use coating color for nose. Shape hat with fondant. For cake, layer rounds from People Pops Sprinkle Set with Pink Candy Melts; attach to Jumbo Confetti plate. Attach jimmy for candle; add flame with Red Candy Melts.

f st. nick on a stick!
Coating: White Candy Melts tinted with orange from Primary Candy Color Set. Pipe in clothes and details with Red, White, Yellow Candy Melts and white candy tinted with black from Garden Candy Color Set. Shape hat with red tinted fondant; pipe pompom with white candy.

g aloha guy
Coating: White tinted with Light Cocoa Candy Melts. Pipe in dress with white candy tinted with green from Garden Candy Color Set; pipe shoes with Yellow and features with Light Cocoa Candy Melts. Attach Jumbo Nonpareils for necklace, daisies and hearts from Flowerful Medley Sprinkles for hem and hair bow.

h catching the wave
Coating: White tinted with Light Cocoa Candy Melts. Pipe in trunks in white tinted with blue from Primary Candy Color Set. Attach flowers from Flowerful Medley Sprinkles. Pipe Light Cocoa features. Shape surfboard with yellow tinted fondant and thread on stick.

i big top treat
Coating: White Candy Melts tinted with orange from Primary Candy Color Set. Pipe in clothes with white candy tinted with blue from Primary Candy Color Set. Pipe hair using orange candy. Shape hat from green tinted fondant. Attach Jumbo Rainbow Nonpareil trim and Confetti from Flowerful Medley Sprinkles.

j alien invasion
Coating: White Candy Melts tinted with yellow and green from Primary and Garden Candy Color Sets. Pipe details in green and yellow; add mouth with white candy tinted with black from Garden Candy Color Set. Attach Candy Eyeball.

k plundering pop
Coating: White Candy Melts tinted with orange from Primary Candy Color Set. Use tinted white candy for all details using yellow, green, violet and black from Primary and Garden Candy Color Sets.

l high sticking
Coating: White Candy Melts tinted with orange from Primary Candy Color Set. Pipe hair with Light Cocoa Candy Melts. Use tinted white candy for remaining details using black and red from Primary and Garden Candy Color Sets. From rolled fondant, cut stick and skate blades; tint portion black and shape puck and gloves.

m cute cowgirl
Coating: White Candy Melts tinted with orange from Primary Candy Color Set. Pipe facial features with Light Cocoa Candy Melts and coating color. Cut and shape clothes and hair with rolled fondant tinted blue, brown and yellow. Attach white circles from People Pops Sprinkles Set for hem, diamond from People Pops Sprinkle Set for buckle.

n cheering you up
Coating: White tinted with Light Cocoa Candy Melts. Pipe hair and facial features with Light Cocoa Candy Melts tinted with black from Garden Candy Color Set and coating color candy. Cut and shape clothes, bow and pompoms with white and violet tinted rolled fondant.

o stylish snowman
Coating: White Candy Melts. Pipe details with White Candy Melts tinted with black from Garden Candy Color Set and orange from Primary Candy Color Set. Shape hat from fondant tinted black and red. Pipe buckle with yellow candy.

p board chairman
Coating: White Candy Melts tinted with orange from Primary Candy Color Set. Pipe hair and facial features with Light Cocoa Candy Melts and coating color candy. Use tinted white candy for clothes using green, blue and red from Primary and Garden Candy Color Sets. Cut skateboard from orange tinted fondant. Attach rounds from People Pops Sprinkle Set for wheels; pipe axles with orange tinted candy.

q drac in black
Coating: White Candy Melts tinted gray with black from Garden Candy Color Set. Use tinted white candy for features and clothes using violet, black and green colors from Garden Candy Color Set. Cut cape with black tinted fondant.

r sun seeker
Coating: White Candy Melts tinted with orange from Garden Candy Color Set. For bikini, attach triangles from Animal Pops Sprinkle Set; for sunglasses, attach hearts from Flowerful Medley Sprinkles. Pipe hair and details with White Candy Melts tinted yellow, pink and black from Primary and Garden Candy Color Sets..

s teddy in tie
Coating: Light Cocoa Candy Melts. Pipe details with various shades of Light Cocoa. For facial features, pipe White Candy Melts tinted with black from Garden Candy Color Set. For tie, attach hearts from Flowerful Medley Sprinkles and Jumbo Nonpareil for knot.

t strongman
Coating: White Candy Melts tinted with orange from Primary Candy Color Set. Pipe in clothes and pipe features with Red Candy Melts and White Candy Melts tinted with black from Garden Candy Color Set. For barbells, insert cut spice drops in black shoestring licorice; secure with candy.

Your favorite personalities start by pressing the Favorite Cake Pops Recipe in our Silicone Boy Mold (2105-0553). Flexible silicone helps the shapes release perfectly!

make it a pops party!

Think small when you're planning your next celebration. You're about to discover that all the fun of a big decorated cake can fit on the end of a stick! In fact, a pop will support any party theme perfectly just by adding a few fun decorating touches. With pops, you can launch a fleet of sailboats, unleash all the animals in the jungle or let fly with bunches of balloons in every color of the rainbow. You won't believe all of the pop options waiting for you—from tea cups to tacos, butterflies to buccaneers. The pops panorama is yours to explore!

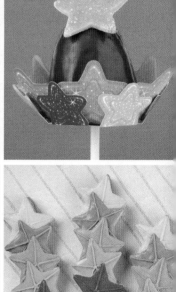

a wrap up a rainbow

PAN
9 x 13 x 2 in. Sheet

RECIPE
Favorite Cake Ball Pops, p. 7

CANDY
White, Yellow, Orange, Lavender Candy Melts,
Garden Candy Color Set (pink, green) Chocolate
Pro Melting Pot

ALSO
White Sparkling Sugar, 6 in. Lollipop Sticks, plastic
wrap, white curling ribbon, scissors

INSTRUCTIONS
Prepare small cake balls and attach stick
following recipe. Tint melted white Candy
Melts pink and green using candy colors.
Dip pops in melted candy; then sprinkle
with Sparkling Sugar. Chill until firm. Cut
5 in. squares of plastic wrap. Insert stick in
center of square, wrap around pop and
twist ends. Tie with ribbon.

b cupcakes reach new heights

PAN
Mini Muffin

TIP
12

CANDY
Green, Pink, Yellow, Blue, Orange Candy Melts,
Chocolate Pro Melting Pot

RECIPE
Buttercream Icing, p. 7

ALSO
Pops Decorating Stand, 8 in. Cookie Treat Sticks, Cinnamon Drops Sprinkles, Parchment Triangles, knife, ruler

INSTRUCTIONS
Bake and cool mini cupcakes. Insert sticks
following Favorite Cake Pops recipe (p. 7).
Chill. Dip in melted candy. Place in Decorating
Stand until set. Use melted candy in cut
parchment bags to pipe zigzags around
bottom. Pipe tip 12 icing swirl over top.
Position cinnamon drop.

c poppy birthday to you

PAN
9 x 13 x 2 in. Sheet, Cooling Grid, Cookie Sheet

CANDY
White, Light Cocoa Candy Melts, Chocolate Pro
Melting Pot

RECIPE
Pound Cake from a Cake Mix, p. 7

ALSO
Jumbo Rainbow Nonpareils, Flowerful Medley
Sprinkles (confetti), Pops Doilies, 101 Cookie Cutters
Set (small round), Pops Decorating Stand, 6 in.
Lollipop Sticks, Parchment Paper, Parchment
Triangles, 9 in. Rolling Pin, yellow spice drops,
granulated sugar, knife, ruler

INSTRUCTIONS
Bake and cool 1¼ in. high cake. Imprint cakes
with small round cutter from set; cut with
knife. Ice bottom with melted candy; chill
until firm. Place on cooling grid over
parchment- covered cookie sheet and cover
with melted candy. Chill until firm. Cut
opening for stick. Insert sticks following pops
recipe (p. 7) leaving 1 in. of stick extended at
top. Chill. Drizzle top with melted white candy
in cut parchment bag; tap to encourage drips.
Use dots of melted candy to secure doily
under cake, attach confetti border and attach
nonpareils to top. Flatten spice drop on
parchment paper sprinkled with granulated
sugar. Cut and shape ⅝ in. high flame. Attach
using melted candy.

a

b

c

d nice slices

PANS
8 x 2 in. Square, Cooling Grid

CANDY
Light Cocoa, White Candy Melts, Primary (yellow), Garden (pink) Candy Color Sets,

RECIPE
Pound Cake from a Cake Mix, p. 7

ALSO
Pops Decorating Stand, Pops Treat Sticks, Pops Doilies, Round Comfort-Grip Cutter, Flowerful Medley Sprinkles (confetti), Cake Board, Parchment Triangles, Parchment Paper, knife, ruler

INSTRUCTIONS
Bake and cool cake. Cut circles using round cutter, then use knife to cut into 6ths. Ice bottoms with melted candy; let set. Place on parchment-covered board and chill until firm. Place on cooling grid over parchment paper. Cover with melted candy; chill until firm. Repeat as needed for smooth surface. Use melted candy in cut parchment bag to pipe icing areas in contrasting color. Let set. Place on parchment. Pipe bead border using melted candy in cut parchment bag. Attach confetti with melted candy. Use tip of knife to poke hole through bottom. Position on doily; attach to treat stick with melted candy.

e sundaes on sticks

PAN
9 x 13 x 2 in. Sheet

CANDY
White (2 pks.), Orange, Yellow, Red, Blue Candy Melts, Garden (pink, green, violet) Candy Color Set, Chocolate Pro Melting Pot

RECIPE
Favorite Cake Ball Pops, p. 7

ALSO
Pops Decorating Stand, Rainbow Nonpareils, Cinnamon Drops Sprinkles, 6 in. Lollipop Sticks, Parchment Triangles; knife, tape, solid vegetable shortening

INSTRUCTIONS
Prepare medium cake balls and insert sticks following recipe. Chill. Dip in melted candy in assorted colors. Place in Decorating Stand; chill until firm. Thin ¼ cup melted white Candy Melts by adding ½ teaspoon shortening. Work with one pop at a time. Use cut parchment bag to pipe topping and drips; immediately sprinkle on nonpareils and position cinnamon drop. Chill until firm.

ⓐ party-ready pops!

PAN
9 x 13 x 2 in. Sheet

COLORS*
Violet, Rose, Leaf Green, Lemon Yellow, Royal Blue

CANDY
White, Yellow Candy Melts, Primary (orange, blue) and Garden (green, black) Candy Color Sets, Chocolate Pro Melting Pot

RECIPE
Favorite Cake Ball Pops, p. 7

ALSO
6 in. Lollipop Sticks, Parchment Triangles, White Ready-To-Use Rolled Fondant (½ oz. per treat), Pops Decorating Stand

INSTRUCTIONS
Prepare small cake balls; chill. Insert sticks following recipe; chill. Dip in melted yellow candy. Place in Decorating Stand; chill until firm. Use melted candy in cut parchment bag to pipe dot eyes and outline mouths. For hats, tint ½ oz. portions of fondant violet, green and blue. Roll a ¾ in. ball in each color and shape into 1½ in. high cones. Attach hats and pipe dot pompom and zigzag brim with melted candy in cut parchment bag.

*Combine Violet and Rose for violet fondant. Combine Leaf Green and Lemon Yellow for green fondant. Tint melted yellow candy with green candy color for green candy shown.

ⓑ lift your gift!

PANS
10.5 x 15.5 x 1 in. Jelly Roll, Cookie Sheet, Cooling Grid

COLORS*
Rose, Sky Blue, Orange, Kelly Green, Lemon Yellow, Golden Yellow

FONDANT
White Ready-To-Use Rolled Fondant (½ oz. per treat), 9 in. Rolling Pin, Roll & Cut Mat, Brush Set; Square Cut-Outs

CANDY*
Orange, Yellow, White Candy Melts, Garden (pink, green), Primary (blue) Candy Color Sets

RECIPE
Pound Cake from a Cake Mix, p. 7

ALSO
Flowerful Medley Sprinkles (confetti), Pops Decorating Stand, Parchment Paper; 6 in. Lollipop Sticks, Cake Leveler; knife; ruler

INSTRUCTIONS
Bake and cool cake; level to 1 in. high. Cut gifts using medium and large Cut-Outs (cut medium into 1¼ in. squares for small gifts; cut large in half for rectangles). Ice bottoms with melted candy; chill until firm on parchment-covered cookie sheet. Place gifts on cooling grid over parchment-covered cookie sheet. Pour on melted, tinted candy to cover. Tap to settle; chill until firm. Cut small hole for stick, dip stick in melted candy and insert. Place in Decorating Stand; chill until firm. Tint fondant darker shades. Roll out ¹⁄₁₆ in. thick. Cut ¼ in. wide strips for ribbon (⅛ in. wide for smallest gift). Attach using damp brush, trimming as needed. Cut matching strips and fold into loops to make bows; attach. Roll small fondant ball, flatten and attach for knot. Attach confetti using melted candy.

*Combine Lemon Yellow with Golden Yellow for yellow fondant shown. Add white candy to orange and yellow candy for lighter shades shown.

Wilto

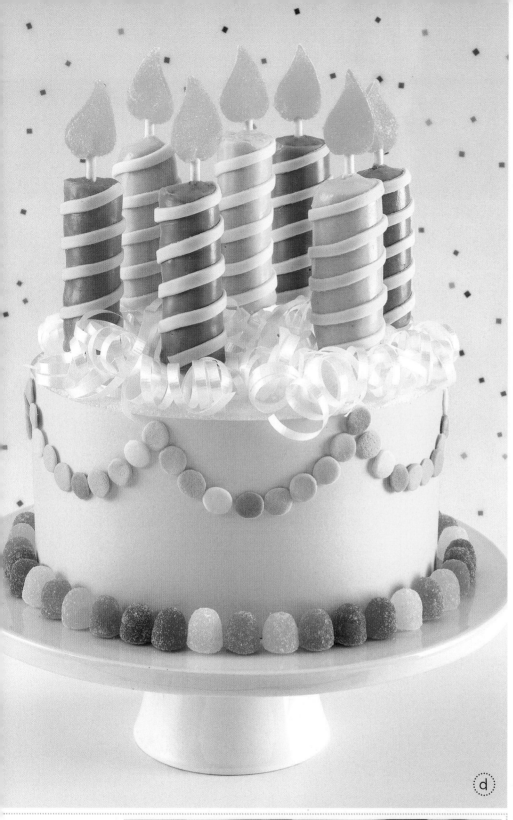

ⓒ bitty bears

PANS
3-D Mini Bear Pan, Cooling Grid

COLORS*
Leaf Green, Orange, Violet, Rose

CANDY
White, Light Cocoa Candy Melts; Garden (black) Candy Color Set, Chocolate Pro Melting Pot

FONDANT
White Ready-To-Use Rolled Fondant (½ oz. per treat), 9 in. Rolling Pin, Roll & Cut Mat

ALSO
6 in. Lollipop Sticks; Parchment Triangles, Disposable Decorating Bags, Parchment Paper; knife

INSTRUCTIONS
Bake and cool cake pops following pan instructions. Insert sticks following Favorite Cake Ball Pops recipe (p. 7); chill. Cover with melted candy using cut disposable bag. Tap to settle; chill until firm. Lighten a small portion of light cocoa candy with a little white; pipe muzzle and let set. Tint cocoa candy black; pipe dot nose, eyes and outline mouth. Let set. Tint ½ oz. portions of fondant green, orange and violet. Roll ½ in. ball; shape a 1 in. high cone hat. ^ttach with melted candy. Roll out remaining fondant ¹⁄₁₆ in. thick. Cut ¹⁄₁₆ in. wide strips; cut pieces to form number. Using melted white candy in cut parchment bag, attach numbers, pipe dot pompom and pull-out brim. Let set.

*Combine Violet with Rose for violet shown.

ⓓ everyone gets their wish

PANS
9 x 13 x 2 in. Sheet

COLORS*
Rose, Violet, Royal Blue, Kelly Green, Lemon Yellow

FONDANT
White Ready-To-Use Rolled Fondant (½ oz. per treat), 9 in. Rolling Pin, Roll & Cut Mat, Brush Set, Leaf Cut-Outs

CANDY
White Candy Melts, Primary (yellow, orange, red, blue), Garden (pink, green, violet) Candy Color Sets

RECIPE
Favorite Cake Ball Pops, p. 7

ALSO
Jumbo Confetti Sprinkles, 8 in. Cookie Treat Sticks, 10 in. Cake Circle, Fanci-Foil Wrap, Hidden Pillars (cut into 3 in. lengths), Parchment Triangles, 4 x 8 in. diameter craft foam circle, large and small spice drops, white curling ribbon (15 to 24 in. lengths), yellow and white construction paper, scissors, knife, ruler, double-sided tape

INSTRUCTIONS
In advance: Prepare cake base. Wrap cake circle in foil. Wrap side of craft foam circle in yellow paper and top in white paper. Secure craft foam to cake circle using melted candy. Divide craft foam circle into 6ths. Decorate using melted candy in cut parchment bag. Attach confetti for garlands, 1 ½ in. deep. Attach small spice drops for bottom border.

Pack cake ball mixture firmly into 7 pillars. Insert sticks all the way through, leaving ¾ in. extended at top. Chill 2 hours or more then push out candle pops. Gently roll in hands to eliminate ridges. Cover pops in melted, tinted candy using cut parchment bag. Tap to settle; chill until firm. Use knife to clean off any excess candy on stick tip. Tint fondant in lighter shades than candy and roll out ¹⁄₁₆ in. thick. Cut a ¼ x 12 in. strip. Brush back with damp brush and attach for spiral trim. For flame, flatten large yellow spice drops. Cut using medium leaf Cut-Out. Push onto stick. Position pops in cake. Scatter curled ribbon to hide sticks.

*Combine Violet with Rose for violet fondant shown.

Smiling faces all around! Cake ball pops topped with colorful fondant party hats trimmed with candy are the sure way for kids to have a nice birthday!

celebrations

the stars are aligned

PANS
Silicone Star Pops Mold, Cookie Sheet, Cooling Grid

CANDY*
White Candy Melts, Primary (yellow, orange, blue, red), Garden (green) Candy Color Sets

RECIPE
Pound Cake from a Mix, p. 7

ALSO
Cookie Treat Sticks, Parchment Triangles, knife, ruler

INSTRUCTIONS
Bake and cool pops in silicone mold supported by cookie sheet; fill cavities ⅔ full and insert sticks before baking. Using melted, tinted candy in cut parchment bags, pipe top, bottom and middle stars; let set. Pipe remaining 2 stars; let set. Pipe outline details using melted candy in cut parchment bag.

*Mix green and yellow candy colors for green candy shown.

(b) stars will dazzle

PANS
Star Pops Cookie Pan, Cookie Sheet, Cooling Grid

RECIPE
Vanilla Sugar Cookies on a Stick, p. 7

ALSO
White Candy Melts, Red, Orange Colored Sugar, 6 in. Cookie Treat Sticks, Brush Set, Cake Boards, Parchment Paper, Parchment Triangles. curling ribbon (18 in. lengths), scissors

INSTRUCTIONS
Prepare cookie dough and press into pan. Bake and cool cookies with sticks. Set on cooling grid over parchment-covered cookie sheet. Pour on melted candy to cover. Tap to settle; place on parchment-covered board and chill until firm. Use melted candy in cut parchment bag to pipe center star. Immediately sprinkle on red sugar; let set then brush away excess. Pipe outer border. Sprinkle on orange sugar; let set then brush away excess. Tie ribbon around stick and curl.

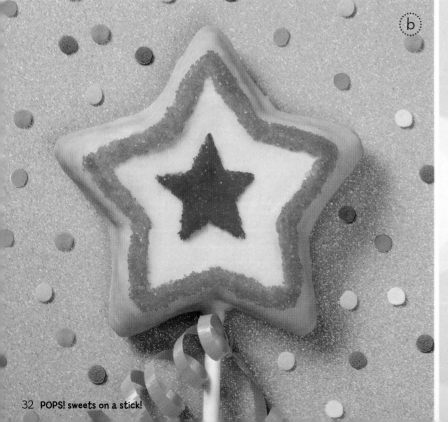

Wilt

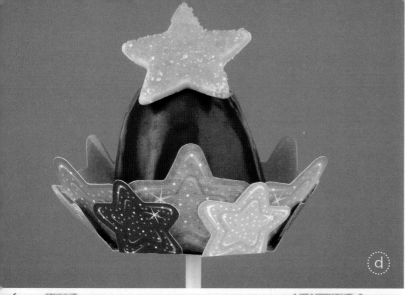

c chews your favorite color

PANS
9 x 13 x 2 in. Sheet; Silicone Round Brownie Pops; Cookie Sheet, Cooling Grid

COLORS
Red-Red, Black

FONDANT
White Ready-To-Use Rolled Fondant (1 oz. per treat), 9 in. Rolling Pin; Roll & Cut Mat; Brush Set

RECIPE
Favorite Cake Ball Pops, p. 7

ALSO
Red Candy Melts, White Candy Dips, Flowerful Medley Sprinkles (confetti), 4 in. Lollipop Sticks, 8 in. Cookie Treat Sticks, 9 in. Spatula, Pops Decorating Stand, Parchment Paper, Piping Gel, knife

INSTRUCTIONS
Prepare small cake balls and insert 4 in. Lollipop sticks following recipe. Chill. Dip in melted Candy Dips. Place in Decorating Stand; chill until firm. Bake and cool brownies in silicone mold supported by cookie sheet. Using spatula, ice bottom with melted candy; chill. Place brownie on cooling grid over parchment- covered cookie sheet. Cover with melted candy; tap to settle, chill until firm. Cut openings at top and bottom with knife. Pipe a line of candy around stick, 2½ in. from top, to form support ring; chill until firm and repeat. Slide brownie onto stick. Remove cake ball from its stick and insert on top of brownie. Secure with melted candy. Tint portions of fondant red and black; attach the following fondant trims with Piping Gel. Roll out fondant ⅛ in. thick. Cut a ½ x ½ in. black dome shape for base opening; attach. Cut a 6 x ¼ in. strip for bottom border; attach. Roll 1½ x ¼ in. diameter red log for trim around opening. Flatten a ⅝ in. ball for top cap and a ¼ in. ball for handle; attach. Attach confetti with melted candy; let set.

d party with the stars

PANS
Silicone Round Brownie Pops Mold, Cookie Sheet, Cooling Grid

COLOR
Leaf Green

FONDANT
White Ready-To-Use Rolled Fondant (¼ oz. per treat), Roll & Cut Mat, 9 in. Rolling Pin, Brush Set, Star Cut-Outs

CANDY
Light Cocoa Candy Melts, Chocolate Pro Melting Pot

ALSO
Hearts and Stars Pops Wraps, Light Green Colored Sugar, Pops Decorating Stand, 6 in. Cookie Treat Sticks, Piping Gel, Cake Boards, Parchment Triangles, Parchment Paper, cornstarch

INSTRUCTIONS
In advance: Make stars. Tint fondant green and roll out ¹⁄₁₆ in. thick. Cut stars using medium Cut-Out. Let dry overnight on parchment-covered board. Brush with Piping Gel and sprinkle on Colored Sugar.

Bake and cool brownie pops in silicone mold supported by cookie sheet. Insert sticks following pops recipe (p. 7). Chill. Dip in melted candy. Place in Decorating Stand; chill until firm. Use melted candy in cut parchment bag to attach star. Let set in stand. Slide wraps onto sticks, securing with candy.

e a box of rainbows

PAN
9 x 13 x 2 in. Sheet

TIP
7 (multiple tips recommended)

COLORS*
Black, Christmas Red, Royal Blue, Kelly Green, Violet, Lemon Yellow, Golden Yellow, Orange, Rose

FONDANT
White Ready-To-Use Rolled Fondant (1 oz. per treat, 6 oz. for base of box), 9 in. Rolling Pin, Roll & Cut Mat, Brush Set

CANDY
Red, Blue, Green, Lavender, Yellow, Orange, White Candy Melts; Primary, Garden Candy Color Sets

RECIPE
Favorite Cake Ball Pops, p. 7

ALSO
Plastic Dowel Rods (cut into 3 in. lengths) , 8 in. Cookie Treat Sticks, Popcorn Treat Boxes, yellow, black, purple, red construction paper, tape, knife, scissors, non-toxic glue stick

INSTRUCTIONS
Prepare cake ball mixture and firmly pack into a 3 in. dowel rod. Insert stick following recipe, letting ¼ in. extend from top end. Chill 2 hours or more. To release, push up bottom of stick through dowel rod. Use matching candy colors to darken melted Candy Melts, and tint white candy pink. Dip treat in melted candy; chill until firm. Use knife to scrape candy from exposed area of stick. For tip, cover narrow opening of tip 7 with tape. Fill with candy; chill until firm. Make a ¼ in. hole for stick. Attach candy tip with melted candy; let set. Tint ½ oz. portions of fondant lighter shades of crayon colors. Roll out ⅛ in. thick. Cut 2 ½ x 3 ¼ in. strips; attach with damp brush. Tint 1 oz. black; roll out ⅛ in. thick. Cut ⅛ x 3¼ in. strips. Use wide end of tip 7 to cut circle; roll into a ⅝ x 1½ in. oval. Attach to crayons with damp brush. Trim scallops from top of treat box; cover with construction paper. Cut letters, number and bottom trim from construction paper; attach. Fill bottom of box 3 in. high with fondant. Insert crayons, trimming sticks as needed.

*Combine Lemon Yellow with Golden Yellow for yellow fondant shown.

ele-phun!

PANS
Round Pops Cookie Pan; Cookie Sheet, Cooling Grid

COLORS
Rose, Sky Blue, Black

FONDANT
White Ready-To-Use Rolled Fondant (3 oz. per treat); 9 in. Rolling Pin; Roll & Cut Mat, Gum-Tex; Brush Set

CANDY
White, Blue Candy Melts; Primary (blue) and Garden (black) Candy Color Sets

RECIPE
Vanilla Sugar Cookies on a Stick, p. 7

ALSO
6 in. Cookie Treat Sticks, Hearts Plastic Nesting Cutter Set, Parchment Triangles, Parchment Paper, Cake Boards, knife, ruler, cornstarch

INSTRUCTIONS
In advance: Make ears and trunk. Add ⅛ teaspoon Gum-Tex to 3 oz. fondant. Tint ½ oz. rose and remainder blue with a little black. Roll out ⅛ in. thick. Cut 2 blue hearts using 4th largest cutter, 2 pink hearts using 3rd largest cutter. Attach pink to blue hearts with damp brush and let dry on cornstarch-dusted board. For trunk, roll a 1⅛ in. ball into a 2¾ in. log; shape with fingers. Indent end with stick and let dry.

Bake and cool cookies with sticks and set on cooling grid over parchment-covered cookie sheet. Add blue candy color to melted blue candy for deeper shade shown. Cover cookies with candy; chill until firm. Using black tinted candy in cut parchment bag, pipe dot eyes and outline smile; chill. Attach ears behind cookie and trunk with melted candy; chill.

pop cats

PAN
9 x 13 x 2 in. Sheet

CANDY
White Candy Melts, Primary (orange, blue, red), Garden (black) Candy Color Sets, Chocolate Pro Melting Pot, Candy Eyeballs

RECIPE
Favorite Cake Ball Pops, p. 7

ALSO
Animal Pops Sprinkle Set, Pops Decorating Stand, 6 in. Lollipop Sticks, Parchment Triangles; ruler

INSTRUCTIONS
Prepare small cake balls and insert sticks following recipe. Chill. Dip in melted, tinted candy. Place in Decorating Stand; chill until firm. Use tinted candy in cut parchment bag to attach Candy Eyeballs or sprinkle eyes, noses and ears; pipe hair Tint candy black to pipe mouths and pupils.

jungle jammin'

PANS
Silicone Round Brownie Pops Mold, Cookie Sheet, Cooling Grid

CANDY*
White Candy Melts, Garden (orange, yellow, pink) Primary (violet, black, blue, green) Candy Color Sets, Chocolate Pro Melting Pot

ALSO
Jungle Pals Pops Fun Pix, 6 in. Cookie Treat Sticks, White Standard Baking Cups, Cake Board, Parchment Paper, Parchment Triangles, Brush Set

INSTRUCTIONS
Bake and cool brownie pops in silicone mold supported by cookie sheet. Insert sticks following pops recipe (p. 7). Chill. Dip in melted candy. Chill until firm on parchment-covered board. Insert picks. Tint ⅓ cup candy for green grass. Add 1 or 2 drops of water to thicken. Immediately pipe grass in baking cup (p. 13). Chill to set then remove paper cup. Attach pops inside grass with melted candy.

*Combine Yellow with Orange candy color for orange shown. Combine Pink with Violet candy color for pink shown. Combine Blue with Green candy colors for blue shown. Combine Yellow with Green candy color for green grass shown.

Wilt

d tracking the wild treats

PAN
9 x 13 x 2 in. Sheet

COLORS
Brown, Christmas Red, Rose, Black, Orange, Kelly Green

FONDANT
White Ready-To-Use Rolled Fondant (1 oz. per treat), Flower, Leaf, Round, Oval, Heart Cut-Outs; Brush Set, Gum-Tex, 9 in. Rolling Pin; Roll & Cut Mat

CANDY*
Orange, Yellow, Light Cocoa, White, Green Candy Melts; Garden (black) Candy Color Set, Chocolate Pro Melting Pot, Candy Eyeballs

RECIPES
Favorite Cake Ball Pops, p. 7; favorite crisped rice cereal treats

ALSO
6 in. Lollipop Sticks, Wave Flower Former Set, Flower Forming Cups, Comfort-Grip Round Cutter; Parchment Triangles; Pops Display Stand, Pops Decorating Stand, Cake Board; pretzel rod, knife, waxed paper, ruler, green construction paper, curling ribbon, scissors, glue stick

INSTRUCTIONS
In advance: Make palm tree top (p. 13).
Prepare medium cake balls. Insert sticks following recipe. Chill. Dip in melted candy. Place in Decorating Stand; chill until firm. Tint portions of fondant to match candy colors. Roll out all ⅛ in. thick; attach the following features with melted candy. **For tiger:** Cut ears using smallest oval Cut-Out; cut in half. Cut ¼ in. triangles for nose and inside ears. **For lion:** Cut mane with largest flower Cut-Out. Cut circle in center with medium round Cut-Out; attach around pop. For ears, roll a ½ in. ball of fondant; cut in half, flatten. For inner ears, roll ³⁄₁₆ in. balls of rose fondant; flatten. Roll a ½ in. tapered log for nose; cut a ¼ in. triangle for end of nose. **For monkey:** Cut 2 ears using medium oval Cut-Out; reposition Cut-Out to cut each ear 1¼ in. long. Trim side edge to conform to pop with medium round Cut-Out; attach. Cut muzzle using small oval Cut-Out; flatten edges to widen slightly and attach. Roll a ¼ in. ball nose. **For elephant:** Cut ears using medium heart Cut-Out, cut inner ears with small heart Cut-Out, flattening to enlarge slightly. Cut off ½ in. at points with medium heart Cut-Out; attach. For trunk, roll a ¾ in. ball into a log; indent end with stick. Score trunk lines with knife. Pipe all animal details using melted candy in cut parchment bag; chill until firm. For tree base, prepare cereal treats in round cutter, pressing to 1¾ in. high. Mark circle with cutter and cut with knife; let set. Cover with green fondant. Insert pretzel rod and attach treetop with melted candy. Roll ½ in. brown balls for coconuts; attach with candy and chill. Position pops and tree on Pops Display Stand. Add curling ribbon, cut out construction paper grass and attach around each tier.

*Combine melted white candy with black candy color for gray shown.

e pets unleashed!

PAN
9 x 13 x 2 in. Sheet

CANDY*
Yellow, White, Light Cocoa Candy Melts, Chocolate Pro Melting Pot

RECIPE
Favorite Cake Ball Pops, p. 7

ALSO
8 in. Lollipop Sticks, Animal Make-A-Face Icing Decorations, Parchment Triangles, Pops Decorating Stand

INSTRUCTIONS
Prepare small cake ball pops and insert sticks following recipe. Dip pops in melted candy. Place in decorating stand; chill until firm. Attach icing decoration facial features and ears with melted candy.

*Add a little White Candy Melts to Light Cocoa for lighter brown shown.

Take the party on safari with a pop centerpiece that features the cuddliest jungle creatures anywhere. Kids will love to choose their own animals and our Pops Display Stand sets the scene perfectly. Just decorate with construction paper and curling ribbon and add a pretzel tree with fondant leaves.

balloons pop & don't drop!

PAN
9 x 13 x 2 in. Sheet

COLORS*
Lemon Yellow, Golden Yellow, Royal Blue, Christmas Red, Orange, Leaf Green

CANDY
White, Light Cocoa, Red, Yellow, Orange Candy Melts, Primary (blue, yellow) and Garden (green) Candy Color Sets, Chocolate Pro Melting Pot

RECIPE
Favorite Cake Ball Pops, p. 7

ALSO
White Ready-To-Use Rolled Fondant, 11¾ in. Lollipop Sticks (2 pks.), Parchment Triangles, Pops Decorating Stand, 3½ x 2½ in. white basket, ½ in. thick craft foam block, craft knife, scissors, toothpick

INSTRUCTIONS
Prepare small cake balls for 24 balloons and 1 head. Insert sticks following recipe. Chill. Dip in melted, tinted candy. Place in decorating stand and chill until firm. Pipe boy's hair and face using melted candy in cut parchment bag; let set. Tint small portions of fondant for balloon knots and hands. Flatten a ⅜ in. ball for each hand; curve and cut slits for fingers with knife. For knots, shape ⅜ in. balls into a teardrop. Flatten bottom and slide onto stick, secure with candy. Imprint ridges with toothpick. Fill bottom ⅔ of basket with fondant. Cut craft block to fit and place in basket. Cut sticks to various lengths and insert. Attach hands with melted candy.

*Combine Lemon Yellow with Golden Yellow for yellow fondant shown. Combine Orange candy with a little White for skin tone shown. Tint White candy with green and yellow candy colors for green shown.

place the face!

PANS
Cookie Sheet, Cooling Grid

CANDY
White, Orange, Primary (blue, yellow), Garden (green, pink) Candy Color Sets

RECIPE
Roll-Out Cookies, p. 7

ALSO
8 in. Lollipop Sticks, People Make-A-Face Icing Decorations, Star Nesting Cutter Set, Round Cut-Outs, Parchment Triangles, Parchment Paper, Cake Board, Pops Decorating Stand

INSTRUCTIONS
In advance: Make shoes. On parchment-covered cake board, pipe ½ x ¾ in. teardrop shapes using melted candy in cut parchment bag. Chill until firm.

Prepare and roll out dough. Cut body using 3rd smallest star cutter and head using medium Cut-Out. Bake and cool. Place cookies on cooling grid over parchment-covered cookie sheet. Cover with melted candy in color of skin tone and clothing; chill until firm. Pipe hands and cuffs using melted candy in cut parchment bag; chill. Attach shoes and print names with melted candy. Attach icing decoration facial features and hair with melted candy; chill. Attach head to body and stick to back of pops with melted candy; chill.

Wilt

c big top clown pop

PAN
9 x 13 x 2 in. Sheet

TIPS
2, 4

COLORS
Black, Lemon Yellow, Royal Blue

FONDANT
White Ready-To-Use Rolled Fondant (½ oz. per treat), 9 in. Rolling Pin, Roll & Cut Mat, Brush Set

CANDY*
Orange, White Candy Melts, Chocolate Pro Melting Pot

RECIPES
Favorite Cake Ball Pops, Royal Icing, p. 7

ALSO
Pops Doilies, 8 in. Cookie Treat Sticks, Cinnamon Drops Sprinkles, Meringue Powder, Parchment Triangles, Pops Decorating Stand; shredded coconut, knife, ruler

INSTRUCTIONS
Prepare large cake balls and insert sticks following recipe. Chill. Dip in melted candy. Place in Decorating Stand; chill until firm. Tint fondant blue for hats (½ oz. per pop). Shape 1¼ x 1½ in. high hat. Attach to pop with melted candy. Attach cinnamon drop nose. Mix small portions of coconut with melted orange candy. Attach to sides and back of head for hair. Decorate using royal icing. Pipe tip 2 dot eyes and outline mouth; pipe tip 4 pull-out hat trims. Slide doily onto stick.

*Combine orange and white candy for skin tone shown.

d wrap party

PAN
9 x 13 x 2 in. Sheet

CANDY
Favorite Candy Melts Colors, Chocolate Pro Melting Pot

RECIPE
Favorite Cake Ball Pops, p. 7

ALSO
Silver and Jewel Tone Foil Wraps, 6 in. Lollipop Sticks, Pops Decorating Stand; card stock, hole punch, ruler, marker, curling ribbon, scissors

INSTRUCTIONS
Prepare medium cake balls and insert sticks following recipe. Chill. Dip in melted candy. Place in Decorating Stand; chill until firm. Wrap pops. Tie on ribbon with 1 x ½ in. name tags.

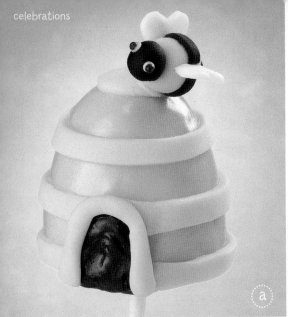

ⓐ beehive brownies

PANS
Silicone Round Brownie Pops Mold, Cookie Sheet, Cooling Grid

TIP
16

COLORS*
Lemon Yellow, Golden Yellow, Black

FONDANT
White Ready-To-Use Rolled Fondant (1 oz. per treat), 9 in. Rolling Pin, Roll & Cut Mat, Brush Set

CANDY
White, Yellow Candy Melts, Garden (black) Candy Color Set, Chocolate Pro Melting Pot

ALSO
Pops Decorating Stand, 6 in. Cookie Treat Sticks, Parchment Triangles; knife, ruler

INSTRUCTIONS
In advance: Make fondant bee. Roll a ½ in. yellow ball body, ¼ in. black ball head. Attach with melted candy. Roll out black and white ⅛ in. thick. For stripe, cut ³⁄₁₆ x 2 in. strip; attach using damp brush. For wings, cut 2 curving shapes, ½ x 1¼ in.; attach using melted candy. Roll tiny flat eyes and ball pupils; attach.

Bake and cool brownies in silicone mold supported by cookie sheet. Melt yellow candy. Dip stick in candy then insert into pop. Chill. Dip in melted candy. Place in Decorating Stand; chill until firm. Use melted, tinted candy in cut parchment bag to pipe doorway; let set. Tint fondant yellow and roll out ⅛ in. thick. Cut 3 strips, ¼ in. wide x 6 in. long, and attach around hive. Roll thin log to wrap around door. Cut top circle using wide end of tip 16. Attach using damp brush. Attach bee using melted candy.

*Combine Lemon Yellow with Golden Yellow for yellow fondant shown.

ⓑ butterfly says hi

PAN
9 x 13 x 2 in. Sheet

FONDANT
Neon Fondant Multi Pack (pink, orange, ½ oz. per treat), Heart Cut-Outs, 9 in. Rolling Pin, Roll & Cut Mat, Brush Set

CANDY
Yellow Candy Melts, Garden (black) Candy Color Set

RECIPE
Favorite Cake Ball Pops, p. 7

ALSO
Flowerful Medley Sprinkles (confetti), 6 in. Lollipop Sticks, Parchment Triangles, Pops Decorating Stand, Parchment Paper; black shoestring licorice, knife, ruler, waxed paper

INSTRUCTIONS
In advance: Make fondant wings. Roll out orange and pink fondant ⅛ in. thick. For each pop, cut 2 orange wings using medium heart Cut-Out and 2 pink wing details using smallest heart Cut-Out. Trim ¼ in. off point of orange wings. Cut pink heart in half and attach using damp brush. Let dry.

Prepare cake balls, 1 each using ½ teaspoon, ¾ teaspoon and 1 teaspoon of mixture for each pop. Stack and insert stick following recipe directions. Chill. Dip in melted candy. Place in Decorating Stand; chill until set. Attach wings to back of pop with melted candy; support with crumpled waxed paper to maintain angle until candy sets. Tint small amount of melted candy black. Use cut parchment bag to pipe eyes and smile. Attach ¾ in. long licorice pieces for antennae. Attach confetti to tip.

ⓒ a worm welcome

PAN
9 x 13 x 2 in. Sheet

TIP
4

COLOR
Black

CANDY*
White Candy Melts, Primary (yellow), Garden (green, black) Candy Color Sets, Chocolate Pro Melting Pot

RECIPES
Favorite Cake Ball Pops, Buttercream Icing, p. 7

ALSO
6 in. Lollipop Sticks, Jumbo Confetti Sprinkles, Flowerful Medley Sprinkles (confetti), Pops Decorating Stand; black shoestring licorice, ruler, knife

INSTRUCTIONS
Prepare medium cake balls and insert sticks following recipe. Chill. D[ip] in melted candy. Place i[n] Decorating Stand; chill until firm. Tint small amount of candy black. Attach jumbo confetti to ⅜ in. lengths of licorice f[or] feet and ¾ in. lengths fo[r] antennae; let set. Use melted candy to attach feet, antennae, confetti nose and spots [on] back. Use tip 4 and buttercream icing to pip[e] eyes (flatten with finger[.] Pipe pupils and smile wi[th] melted candy.

*Tint melted white candy lime green usin[g] yellow and green candy color.

d ladybugs landing

ANS
x 13 x 2 in. Sheet, Cookie Sheet, Cooling
rid

P
A

OLOR
lack

ONDANT
Vhite Ready-To-Use Rolled Fondant
4 oz. per treat), 9 in. Rolling Pin, Brush
et, Gum-Tex

ANDY
White, Red, Yellow, Orange Candy Melts,
arden (black) Candy Color Set, Choc-
ate Pro Melting Pot

ECIPE
avorite Cake Ball Pops, p. 7

LSO
ps Display Stand, 6 in. Lollipop Sticks,
archment Triangles, Parchment Paper,
ake Boards; knife, ruler, scissors, green
onstruction paper, curling ribbon, glue
rick

STRUCTIONS
advance: Make heads. Tint 8 oz.
ndant black and add ½ teaspoon
um-Tex. Roll ¾ in. diameter balls. Let dry
vernight on parchment-covered boards.
eserve remaining fondant.

epare large cake balls and cut in half. Ice
t bottoms with melted candy; let set.
ace candy iced side down on cooling grid
ver parchment-covered cookie sheet. Pour
n melted candy to cover. Tap to settle, chill
ntil set. Attach heads with melted candy;
t set. Tint fondant black and roll out
16 in. thick. Cut spots using narrow end of
2A; attach using damp brush. Use
elted candy in cut parchment bag to pipe
ves, pupils and smiles. Use knife tip to
oke hole in bottom; insert stick and secure
ith melted candy. Trim sticks to various
eights and position pops in stand. Cut
nstruction paper to fit around edge of
ch tier and attach. Add curling ribbon.

e sunny stingers

PAN
9 x 13 x 2 in. Sheet

TIP
1

COLOR
Black

CANDY
Yellow Candy Melts, Chocolate Pro Melting Pot

RECIPES
Favorite Cake Ball Pops, Royal Icing, p. 7

ALSO
Jumbo Heart Sprinkles, Jumbo Flower Sprinkles,
Chocolate Jimmies, Pops Decorating Stand, 6 in.
Cookie Treat Sticks, Parchment Triangles,
Meringue Powder; knife, ruler

INSTRUCTIONS
Prepare small cake balls and insert sticks
following recipe. Chill. Dip in melted candy.
Place in Decorating Stand; chill until firm. Use
black royal icing to pipe tip 1 zigzag stripes
around pop, dot eyes and outline mouth. Use
melted candy in cut parchment bag to attach
heart wings and stinger, jimmy and blossom
antennae.

www.wilton.com

ⓐ pet pops

PAN
9 x 13 x 2 in. Sheet

COLORS*
Black, Golden Yellow, Rose, Brown, Red-Red

FONDANT
White Ready-To-Use Rolled Fondant (½ oz. per treat), Brush Set

CANDY*
Light Cocoa, Yellow, White Candy Melts, Chocolate Pro Melting Pot

RECIPE
Favorite Cake Ball Pops, p. 7

ALSO
Pops Decorating Stand, Primary Colors Fine Tip FoodWriter Edible Color Markers (black), 6 in. Lollipop Sticks; knife, ruler

INSTRUCTIONS
Prepare medium cake balls and insert sticks following recipe. Chill. Dip in melted candy. Place in Decorating Stand; chill until firm. Tint fondant black, brown, yellow and rose. Shape ½ in. triangular cat ears and ¼ in. inside ears; attach with melted candy. Shape flattened oval dog ears, 1¼ in. long x ⅝ in. wide; attach. Shape and flatten cheeks; attach. Shape ball eyes, noses, dog mouth and lower lip; attach. Draw dot whiskers with marker.

*Combine Brown with Red-Red and Black for brown fondant shown. Add white to light cocoa candy for brown shown.

ⓑ delish fish

PAN
9 x 13 x 2 in. Sheet

COLOR
Sky Blue

FONDANT
White Ready-To-Use Rolled Fondant (½ oz. per treat), Brush Set

CANDY
White Candy Melts, Primary (blue, orange, red) Candy Color Set, Chocolate Pro Melting Pot

RECIPE
Favorite Cake Ball Pops, p. 7

ALSO
Rainbow Nonpareils Sprinkles, 6 in. Lollipop Sticks, Parchment Triangles, Pops Decorating Stand; knife, ruler

INSTRUCTIONS
Prepare large cake balls and insert sticks following recipe. Chill. Dip in melted candy tinted blue and press bottom ⅓ with nonpareils. Place in Decorating Stand; chill until firm. Tint fondant to match blue candy. Roll a 4 x ³⁄₁₆ in. log and attach for rim. Tint small amount of candy orange and black (combine red and blue to make black). Use cut parchment bag to pipe oval body of fish. Pipe mouth and fins. Pipe dot eye and bubbles; let set.

Wilt

c barnyard buddies

PAN
x 13 x 2 in. Sheet

COLORS*
ed-Red, Golden Yellow, Orange, Terra Cotta, Brown

FONDANT
White Ready-To-Use Rolled Fondant (½ oz. per treat), 9 in. Rolling
n, Roll & Cut Mat, Brush Set

CANDY
White, Light Cocoa, Pink, Yellow Candy Melts, Garden (black)
andy Color Set, Chocolate Pro Melting Pot

RECIPE
avorite Cake Ball Pops, p. 7

ALSO
ops Decorating Stand, 6 in. Lollipop Sticks; scissors, ruler, knife,
othpicks, scissors

INSTRUCTIONS
repare medium cake balls and insert sticks following recipe. Chill.
p in melted candy. Place in Decorating Stand; chill until firm. Tint
ndant as needed. Shape pieces by hand and attach using damp
rush. **For rooster and chick:** Shape ⅜ in. long beak (indent edge
ith knife), ½ in. flat feet (cut slits and separate toes), 1 in. long x
in. wide flattened wings (slit with scissors), ½ in. flat tail feathers
d ½ x ¾ in. high comb (cut away sections for spike effect). **For
g:** Shape and slightly flatten ⅜ in. balls for feet, ½ in. ball for nose.
ape ⅜ in. pointed ears, 1½ in. long thin log for tail (wrap around
othpick to curl). **For cow:** Shape and flatten ½ in. balls for feet, ⅝
. ball for nose. Shape ⅜ in. pointed ears, 1/16 in. thick irregular white
eces for spots. Using tinted black candy, pipe tiny ball eyes and
ostrils and outline mouth.

ombine Brown with Red-Red for brown fondant shown.

d turtlely cool!

PAN
9 x 13 x 2 in. Sheet

COLORS
Moss Green, Black

FONDANT
White Ready-To-Use Rolled Fondant (¼ oz. per treat),
9 in. Rolling Pin, Roll & Cut Mat, Brush Set, Round
Cut-Outs

CANDY*
White, Dark Green Candy Melts, Garden (black, green)
Candy Color Set, Candy Eyeballs, Chocolate Pro Melting
Pot

RECIPE
Favorite Cake Ball Pops, p. 7

ALSO
Pops Decorating Stand, 6 in. Lollipop Sticks,
Parchment Triangles; large and small chocolate
nougat roll candies, knife, ruler

INSTRUCTIONS
Prepare large cake balls; cut ¼ in. off for flat bottom.
Insert sticks following recipe. Chill. Dip in melted green
candy. Place in Decorating Stand until set. Tint fondant
light green and roll out 1/16 in. thick. Cut circles using
smallest Cut-Out. Attach to turtle using melted candy.
For feet, cut small nougat roll to 3/16 in. high; attach
with melted candy. For head, roll 1 segment of large
nougat into a ball; attach. Attach candy eyes. Pipe
smile using melted candy in cut parchment bag.

*Add green candy color to green candy for green shown.

e school's out!

PAN
9 x 13 x 2 in. Sheet

COLORS*
Orange, Lemon Yellow, Golden Yellow, Rose, Leaf Green

FONDANT
White Ready-To-Use Rolled Fondant (1 oz. per treat), 9 in. Rolling Pin,
Roll & Cut Mat, Brush Set, Heart Cut-Outs

CANDY
White Candy Melts, Garden (pink, green), Primary (yellow, orange)
Candy Color Sets, Candy Eyeballs, Chocolate Pro Melting Pot

RECIPE
Favorite Cake Ball Pops, p. 7

ALSO
Pops Decorating Stand, 6 in. Lollipop Sticks, Gum-Tex; knife, ruler,
spatula

INSTRUCTIONS
In advance: Make fondant trims. Knead ½ teaspoon Gum-Tex into 4 oz.
fondant. Divide into 4 portions and tint orange, yellow, rose and green.
Roll out ⅛ in. thick. Cut lips, top and side fins using smallest heart
Cut-Out. Score lines using edge of spatula. Trim top fin with curved
edge to fit pop. Cut tail fin using medium Cut-Out. Score lines with
spatula. Trim tip and top edge. Let dry overnight.

Prepare small cake balls and insert sticks following recipe. Chill. Dip in
melted tinted candy. Place in Decorating Stand; chill until firm. Cut slits
where lips, top fin and tail will sit. Attach eyes and fondant trims using
melted candy.

*Combine Lemon Yellow with Golden Yellow for yellow fondant shown. Combine Leaf Green with Lemon Yellow for
green fondant shown. Combine yellow and green candy colors for lime green candy shown.

These satchels are a snap! Serve them in 2 fun shapes and mix up the colors and details with a rainbow of fondant.

(a) little sweethearts

PANS
Silicone Round Brownie Pops Mold; Non-Stick Cookie Sheet

CANDY
White Candy Melts, Decorator Brush Set

RECIPE
Pound Cake from a Cake Mix, p. 7

ALSO
Pink Colored Sugar, Jumbo Confetti, Flowerful Medley Sprinkles (confetti), Pops Treat Sticks, Parchment Triangles, Piping Gel, Hearts Nesting Cutter Set, scissors

INSTRUCTIONS
In advance: Mold candy heart. Place smallest heart cutter on cookie sheet. Fill ¼ in. deep with melted candy; chill until firm and unmold. Brush with Piping Gel. Sprinkle with pink sugar.

Bake and cool cakes in mold supported by cookie sheet. Insert stick in treat. Trim ¼ in. off one side of Jumbo Confetti; attach for bottom border with melted candy. Attach small confetti to border and heart to top of treat with melted candy.

(b) carousel creations

PANS
Cookie Sheet, Cooling Grid

TIP
3

COLORS*
Rose, Violet, Lemon Yellow, Golden Yellow

RECIPES
Roll-Out Cookies, Color Flow Icing, p. 7

ALSO
Animal Pals 50-Piece Cutter Set (horse), Pops Decorating Stand, White Candy Melts, 8 in. Lollipop Sticks, Color Flow Mix, Fine Tip Primary Colors FoodWriter Edible Markers (black); gum balls, ⅛ in. wide ribbon (pink, violet, yellow; 12 in. per treat), knife, ruler, cornstarch

INSTRUCTIONS
Prepare and roll out dough. Cut using horse cutter from set. Bake and cool cookies. Outline using tip 3 and full-strength color flow icing; flow in using thinned icing. Let dry 24 hours. Attach ribbon to sticks with melted candy. Attach horse using melted candy; let set. Decorate with tip 3 and full-strength color flow in assorted colors. Pipe outline mane, tail and dot hooves. Outline and fill in saddle center (pat smooth with finger dipped in cornstarch). Pipe outline bridle and saddle edging. Draw dot eye. Use tip of knife to poke hole in gum ball. Push onto top of stick.

*Combine Violet with Rose for violet shown. Combine Lemon Yellow with Golden Yellow for yellow shown.

(c) the tea set

PAN
9 x 13 x 2 in. Sheet

COLOR
Rose

FONDANT
White Ready-To-Use Rolled Fondant (2 oz. per treat), 9 in. Rolling Pin, Roll & Cut Mat, Brush Set, Gum-Tex, Round Cut-Outs

CANDY
White Candy Melts, Garden (pink) Candy Color Set, Chocolate Pro Melting Pot

RECIPE
Favorite Cake Ball Pops, p. 7

ALSO
Pops Decorating Stand, 6 in. Lollipop Sticks, Parchment Triangles; knife, ruler

INSTRUCTIONS
In advance: Make saucers. Tint 2 oz. fondant and add ¼ teaspoon Gum-Tex. Roll out ¹⁄₁₆ in. thick. Cut rounds using medium Cut-Out. Make hole with end of lollipop stick. Let dry overnight. Reserve remaining fondant.

Prepare cake ball mixture. Roll 1 large ball for teapot. For cups, roll small balls and flatten tops. Insert sticks following recipe. Chill. Dip in melted tinted candy. Place in Decorating Stand; chill until firm. Tint small amount of candy darker pink. Use melted candy in cut parchment bag to pipe bead flower petals; add white dot center. For teacups, roll ⅛ x 1 in. fondant logs; shape handles and attach using damp brush. Slide saucers onto sticks and secure with damp brush. For teapot, roll ⅛ x 1¼ in. fondant log; shape handle and attach. Shape and attach 1 x ⅜ in. diameter spout, 1 x ⅜ in. high dome-shaped lid and tiny ball knob.

d cute carry-alls

PANS
Silicone Bite-Size Brownie Squares Mold, Cookie Sheet, Cooling Grid

COLORS*
Rose, Violet, Lemon Yellow, Golden Yellow, Leaf Green, Orange

FONDANT
White Ready-To-Use Rolled Fondant (½ oz. per treat), 9 in. Rolling Pin, Roll & Cut Mat, Brush Set, Round Cut-Outs, Gum-Tex

CANDY*
White, Yellow Candy Melts, Garden (pink) Candy Color Set

RECIPE
Favorite Cake Ball Pops, p. 7

ALSO
Flowerful Medley Sprinkles (confetti), 6 in. Lollipop Sticks, Parchment Paper; knife, ruler

INSTRUCTIONS
Prepare cake ball mixture. For square pops, press into silicone mold. Chill, then unmold. For semicircles, press mixture into large round Cut-Out, filling to top. Chill, unmold then cut in half. Insert sticks following pops recipe. Set on cooling grid over parchment-lined cookie sheet. Cover with melted, tinted candy. Tap to settle, chill until firm. For flaps, roll out fondant ¹⁄₁₆ in. thick. Use smallest round Cut-Out to cut round flap. Cut 1¼ x 2 in. rectangle for pointed flap. Attach using damp brush. Use knife to trim sides and cut point. For yellow purse, cut ¹⁄₁₆ in. wide strips; attach with damp brush. For pink purse, attach confetti with candy. For buttons, roll ³⁄₁₆ in. balls; flatten and attach with damp brush. Make handles. Add ⅛ teaspoon Gum-Tex per 1 oz. fondant; divide and tint. Roll ¼ x 2½ in. diameter logs and curve into U-shape. Lay pops flat on parchment paper and attach handles with melted candy. Chill until firm.

*Combine Violet with Rose for violet fondant shown. Combine Lemon Yellow with Golden Yellow for yellow fondant shown. Mix white and yellow candy for yellow candy shown.

POPS! sweets on a stick! 43

a crowned heads

PAN
9 x 13 x 2 in. Sheet

TIPS
1, 4

COLORS
Lemon Yellow, Royal Blue, Pink, Moss Green, Black

FONDANT
White Ready-To-Use Rolled Fondant (½ oz. per treat), 9 in. Rolling Pin, Roll & Cut Mat, Brush Set

CANDY*
White, Light Cocoa Candy Melts, Primary (orange) Candy Color Set, Chocolate Pro Melting Pot

RECIPES
Favorite Cake Ball Pops, Buttercream Icing, p. 7

ALSO
Green, Blue, Pink, Yellow Sugar Pearls, White Pearl Dust, Imitation Clear Vanilla Extract, 6 in. Lollipop Sticks, Pops Decorating Stand; knife, ruler

INSTRUCTIONS
Prepare medium cake balls and insert sticks following recipe. Chill. Dip in melted candy tinted in desired skin tone. Place in Decorating Stand; chill until firm. Tint fondant assorted colors for crowns (½ oz. per pop); roll out ⅛ in. thick. Cut ½ x 1 in. crowns; attach to pops with melted candy. Paint with Pearl Dust/vanilla mixture; attach Sugar Pearls with tip 1 icing dots. Use icing to pipe tip 4 outline, zigzag and e-motion hair. Pipe tip 1 smile and dot eyes. Pipe nose with a dot of melted candy.

*Add orange candy color to melted white candy for light skin tone shown; add white candy to light cocoa candy for darker skin tones shown.

b princesses on parade

PANS
Silicone Round Brownie Pops Mold, Cookie Sheet, Cooling Grid

TIPS
1, 2, 101s

COLORS*
Rose, Violet, Lemon Yellow

CANDY
White Candy Melts, Garden (pink, violet) Candy Color Set, Chocolate Pro Melting Pot

RECIPE
Royal Icing, p. 7

ALSO
Princess Pops Fun Pix, Pops Decorating Stand, 6 in. Cookie Treat Sticks, Parchment Triangles; knife, ruler, toothpicks

INSTRUCTIONS
Bake and cool brownie pops in silicone mold supported by cookie sheet. Insert sticks following pops recipe. Chill. Dip in melted candy. Place in Decorating Stand until set. Divide base into 8ths. Use royal icing to pipe tip 101s zigzag scallops (½ in. deep) around bottom. Pipe tip 2 dots at top of scallop; pipe tip 1 dots on dress. Cut slit for picks and insert picks.

*Combine Rose with Lemon Yellow for pink icing shown. Combine Violet with Rose for violet icing shown. Combine violet with pink for the violet candy color shown.

Wilt

Princess pops rule! The Round Brownie Pops Mold creates the ideal skirt shape—top it with candy ruffles and polka dot trim, then add the cute princess pick.

c the royal ballet

PANS
9 x 13 x 2 in. Sheet, Cookie Sheet, Cooling Grid

COLORS*
Ivory, Brown, Rose

FONDANT
White Ready-To-Use Rolled Fondant (¼ oz. per treat), 9 in. Rolling Pin, Roll & Cut Mat, Brush Set

CANDY
White Candy Melts, Garden (pink) Candy Color Set

RECIPE
Favorite Cake Ball Pops, p. 7

ALSO
Princess Pops Fun Pix, White Mini Baking Cups, Pastry Brush, Pops Decorating Stand, 11¾ in. Lollipop Sticks, Parchment Paper, Parchment Triangles; knife, ruler

INSTRUCTIONS

In advance: Make skirt. Partially flatten baking cup. Use pastry brush to brush on melted tinted candy; chill until firm. Remove baking cup.

Prepare small cake balls and cut in half; chill. Ice flat bottom with candy; chill. Set iced side down on cooling grid over parchment-covered cookie sheet. Pour on melted candy to cover. Tap to settle; chill until firm. Tint fondant and shape 1½ in. long legs over stick, beginning 1 in. from top. Use knife to indent center. Use tip of knife to cut hole in pop bottom and skirt; slide onto stick and secure with candy. Pipe shoes with melted candy in cut parchment bag. For belt, roll a ¼ x 3 in. fondant log; attach using damp brush. Cut 2 small triangles for bow; roll a tiny ball for knot. Attach. Cut a slit for pick and insert, securing with melted candy.

*Combine Ivory with Brown for skin tone shown.

d her chariot awaits

PANS
Round Cookie Pops Pan, Cookie Sheet, Cooling Grid

TIPS
1, 3

COLORS
Rose, Brown, Red-Red, Copper (for skin tone shown), Black

FONDANT
White Ready-To-Use Rolled Fondant (4 oz. per treat), 9 in. Rolling Pin, Roll & Cut Mat, Brush Set, Gum-Tex, Round Cut-Outs

RECIPES
Vanilla Sugar Cookies on a Stick, Color Flow Icing, p. 7

ALSO
Comfort-Grip Flower Cutter, White Cake Sparkles, Color Flow Mix, Piping Gel, 8 in. Cookie Treat Sticks, Parchment Paper, Parchment Triangles; knife, ruler

INSTRUCTIONS

In advance: Prepare carriage trims. Tint 4 oz. fondant rose and add ¼ teaspoon Gum-Tex. Roll out ⅛ in. thick. Cut 2 wheels using medium Cut-Out. Use cutter to cut flower for roof trim; use knife to trim to just 3 petals, matching curve of carriage roof. Let dry 2 days.

Prepare cookie dough and press into pan with 8 in. sticks. Bake and cool following pan directions. Set cookies on cooling grid over parchment-covered cookie sheet. Pour on thinned color flow icing to cover. Tap to settle; let set. Use full-strength icing to outline door and window; flow in with thinned icing. Let dry. Use Piping Gel in cut parchment bag to decorate carriage and to outline roof trim and wheels; immediately sprinkle on Cake Sparkles. Attach trim and wheels with full-strength icing. Support until set. Pipe tip 3 bead flowers. Tint fondant in desired skin tone; roll out ⅛ in. thick. Cut head using wide end of tip 3; attach using damp brush. Pipe tip 3 crown, outline door edge and handle, dot flower centers. Pipe tip 1 curly hair, dot eyes and outline smile.

*Combine Brown with Red-Red for brown shown.

filigree flowers

PANS
Silicone Round Brownie Pops Mold;
Non-Stick Cookie Sheet

COLOR
Leaf Green

FONDANT
White Ready-To-Use Rolled Fondant (½ oz.
per treat), 9 in. Rolling Pin, Roll & Cut Mat,
Brush Set, Flower, Leaf Cut-Outs, Gum-Tex

ALSO
Pink, Yellow, Lavender Colored Sugars, 6 in.
Cookie Treat Sticks, Jumbo Confetti
Sprinkles, Wave Flower Former Set, White
Candy Melts, Parchment Triangles, Piping
Gel, Pops Decorating Stand, toothpick,
cornstarch

INSTRUCTIONS
In advance: Make leaves. Knead ⅛ teaspoon Gum-Tex in 2 oz. fondant; tint
green. Roll out ⅛ in. thick; cut one leaf
for each treat using medium Cut-Out.
Score veins using toothpick. Let dry on
cornstarch-dusted Wave Flower Former.

Bake and cool brownie pops in silicone
mold supported by cookie sheet; unmold.
Dip stick in melted candy and insert in
bottom of pop. Position medium flower
Cut-Out on cookie sheet. Fill ¼ in. thick
with melted candy; chill until firm and
unmold. Repeat for additional flowers.
Brush flowers with Piping Gel; cover with
colored sugar. Attach jumbo confetti
center with melted candy. Use melted candy in
cut parchment bag to pipe scrolls on sides
of pops; let set 1 minute then sprinkle with
sugar. Attach candy flower with melted
candy. Attach leaf to bottom with candy.

garden treasures

PANS
Silicone Round Brownie Pops Mold, Cookie
Sheet, Cooling Grid

COLORS*
Rose, Golden Yellow, Lemon Yellow, Royal
Blue, Sky Blue, Leaf Green

FONDANT
White Ready-To-Use Rolled Fondant (1 oz.
per treat), 9 in. Rolling Pin, Roll & Cut Mat,
Brush Set, Leaf Cut-Outs

CANDY
White Candy Melts, Garden (pink), Primary
(blue, yellow) Candy Color Sets

RECIPES
Pound Cake from a Cake Mix, p. 7; Spritz
Cookies (from Cookie Pro Ultra II Cookie
Press instructions)

ALSO
Cookie Pro Ultra II Cookie Press (daisy),
White Nonpareils, Imitation Clear Vanilla
Extract, Pops Decorating Stand, 11¾ in.
Lollipop Sticks, Cake Boards, Parchment
Paper, Parchment Triangles; mini
candy-coated chocolate dots, knife, ruler

INSTRUCTIONS
In advance: Make cookies. Prepare spritz
dough. Press out daisies. Bake and cool.
Pipe in petals using melted white candy in
cut parchment bag; immediately sprinkle
on nonpareils. Attach candy dot to center.
Let set.

Bake and cool pops in silicone mold
supported by cookie sheet. Trim flat side to
level; ice with melted, tinted candy. Set iced
side down on parchment-covered board;
chill until set. Set on cooling rack over
parchment-covered cookie sheet. Pour on
candy to cover. Tap to settle, chill until set.
Pipe a support ring around sticks, about 4 in.
from top, using melted candy in cut parchment bag. Let set then overpipe. Chill. Use
knife tip to poke holes in pot; slide onto stick.
Secure to ring support using melted candy.
For pot trims, tint fondant and roll out ⅛ in.
thick. Cut ¼ in. wide strips (8 at 2 in. long,
1 at 6 in. long). Attach using damp brush,
trimming as needed. Paint top of stick with
vanilla tinted green. Tint fondant green and
roll out ⅛ in. thick. Cut leaves using smallest
Cut-Out. Attach leaves and cookie flower to
stick using melted candy.

**Combine Golden Yellow with Lemon Yellow for yellow shown.
Combine Royal Blue with Sky Blue for blue shown.*

pops & posies

PANS
Silicone Round Brownie Pops Mold, Cookie
Sheet, Cooling Grid

COLOR
Rose

FONDANT
White Ready-To-Use Rolled Fondant
(¼ oz. per treat); 9 in. Rolling Pin; Roll & Cut
Mat, Brush Set, Flower Cut-Outs, Fondant
Shaping Foam, 10 Pc. Fondant/Gum Paste
Tool Set

CANDY
Light Cocoa, White Candy Melts, Garden
(pink) Candy Color Set, Candy Melting
Plate, Chocolate Pro Melting Pot

ALSO
Ruffle Pops Wraps, Pops Decorating Stand,
6 in. Lollipop Sticks, Parchment Triangles;
cornstarch, ruler

INSTRUCTIONS
In advance: Make flowers. Tint fondant
and roll out ¹⁄₁₆ in. thick. Cut flowers using
medium Cut-Out. Place on foam and
indent centers using large end of ball tool.
Set in Candy Melting Plate dusted with
cornstarch. Roll ³⁄₁₆ in. diameter ball
centers; attach using damp brush. Let
dry overnight.

Bake and cool brownie pops in silicone
mold supported by cookie sheet. Insert
sticks following pops recipe (p. 7). Chill. Dip
in melted candy. Place in Decorating Stand;
chill until firm. Use melted, tinted candy in
cut parchment bag to pipe spiral and attach
flower. Let set in stand. Slide wraps onto
sticks, securing with melted candy.

(d)

(d) bright-eyed blooms

PAN
...ower Pops Cookie Pan, Cookie Sheet, Cooling Grid
...P

COLORS
...se, Lemon Yellow, Black

RECIPES
...anilla Sugar Cookies on a Stick, Color Flow Icing, p. 7

ALSO
...andy Eyeballs, Pink Colored Sugar, Color Flow Mix,
...rchment Paper, 8 in. Cookie Treat Sticks; knife, ruler

INSTRUCTIONS
...epare dough and press into pops cavities with sticks.
...ake and cool. Place on cooling grid over parchment-
...vered cookie sheet. Thin icing and tint. Pour over
...okies to cover. Sprinkle on colored sugar. Let dry
...vernight. Use tip 2 and full-strength icing to pipe 1¾ in.
...ameter face; flow in using thinned icing. Let dry. Use
... 2 and full-strength icing to attach eyes and to pipe
...utline smile and dot cheeks (flatten with finger).

(e) potted pops

PANS
...ower Pops Cookie Pan, Cookie Sheet, Cooling Grid

COLORS
...af Green, Lemon Yellow, Rose, Violet, Orange

CANDY
...hite, Yellow Candy Melts, Primary (orange), Garden
...ink, green, violet) Candy Color Sets

RECIPE
...anilla Sugar Cookies on a Stick, p. 7

ALSO
...ops Flower Pot Kit; Light Green, Orange, Pink,
...avender, Yellow Colored Sugars, 8 in. Cookie Treat
...icks, Metal Spatula, Parchment Paper, Parchment
...iangles; knife, ruler, curling ribbon, 2 in. wide pink
...bbon (2 ft. in length)

INSTRUCTIONS
...epare dough and press into pops cavities with sticks.
...ake and cool. Place on cooling grid over parchment-
...vered cookie sheet. Pour on melted, tinted candy to
...ver. Tap to settle; chill until firm. Pipe on petal details
...work with 1 or 2 petals at a time) using melted candy
... cut parchment bag; immediately sprinkle on
...atching colored sugar. Let set. Use hot spatula to
...elt flat side of yellow candy disk; immediately
...rinkle on yellow sugar. Attach to center with melted
...ndy. Assemble flower pot and insert pops. Position
...rling ribbon and bow.

(e)

b little leaguers

PAN
9 x 13 x 2 in. Sheet

TIP
1

CANDY
White, Light Cocoa Candy Melts, Primary (yellow, red, blue, orange), Garden (black) Candy Color Sets, Truffles Candy Mold, Chocolate Pro Melting Pot

RECIPE
Favorite Cake Ball Pops, p. 7

ALSO
Pops Decorating Stand, 6 in. Lollipop Sticks, Parchment Paper, Parchment Triangles, Decorator Brush Set; measuring spoons, knife, ruler, tape

INSTRUCTIONS
In advance: Make candy caps. Tint candy and fill truffles mold using cut parchment bag. Tap to settle; chill until firm. Use ¼ teaspoon measuring spoon to scoop out ¼ in. deep depression accommodate curve of head. Set on parchment-covered surface Pipe 1 x ⅜ in. high brim; smooth seam with brush. Chill until firm Pipe team initial.

Prepare small cake balls and insert sticks following recipe. Chill. Dip in melted candy tinted to desired skin tone. Place in Decorating Stand; chill until set. Tape tip 1 to outside of parchment ba Use melted candy to pipe facial features and various hair styles. Attach caps.

a nothing but net!

PANS
10.5 x 15.5 x 1 in. Jelly Roll, Cookie Sheet, Cooling Grid

TIP
83

COLORS*
Christmas Red, Red-Red

FONDANT
White Ready-To-Use Rolled Fondant (½ oz. per treat), 9 in. Rolling Pin, Brush Set, Square, Round Cut-Outs

CANDY*
White Candy Melts, Primary (orange, red), Garden (black) Candy Color Sets

RECIPE
Roll-Out Cookies, Pound Cake from a Cake Mix, p. 7

ALSO
8 in. Cookie Treat Sticks, Parchment Paper, Parchment Triangles; knife, ruler

INSTRUCTIONS
In advance: Make cookie backboards. Prepare and roll out dough. Cut using largest square Cut-Out. Bake and cool. Place on cooling grid over parchment-covered cookie sheet. Pour on melted white candy to cover. Tap to settle, chill until firm. Use melted red candy in cut parchment bag to pipe border. Let set.

Bake and cool cake; trim to ¾ in. high. Cut rounds for basketballs using medium Cut-Out. Ice bottoms with candy; chill until firm. Place iced side down on cooling grid over parchment-covered cookie sheet. Pour on melted candy to cover. Tap to settle; chill until firm. Pipe black outines using melted candy in cut parchment bag. For net, roll out fondant ⅛ in. thick. Cut a 4 x 1⅜ in. rectangle; cut out holes using tip 83. Wrap and attach around ball, trimming as needed. Attach to backboard using melted candy; let set. For rim, roll out red fondant ⅛ in. thick. Cut a ³/₁₆ x 4 in. strip; attach using damp brush. Attach stick to back of cookie using melted candy.

*Combine Christmas Red with Red-Red for red fondant shown. Tint white candy with orange, black and red candy colors for basketball shade shown.

Wilt

c high pop-up!

PAN
9 x 13 x 2 in. Sheet

TIP
1

CANDY
White, Red Candy Melts, Chocolate Pro Melting Pot

RECIPE
Favorite Cake Ball Pops, p. 7

ALSO
Pops Decorating Stand, 6 in. Lollipop Sticks, Parchment Triangles; knife, ruler, tape

INSTRUCTIONS
Prepare medium cake balls and insert sticks following recipe directions. Chill. Dip in melted white candy. Place in Decorating Stand; chill until firm. Tape tip 1 to outside of cut parchment bag. Pipe seam then stitches using melted red candy. Let set.

d gridiron great

PAN
3-D Mini Bear Pan, Cooling Grid, Cookie Sheet

CANDY*
White, Light Cocoa, Orange Candy Melts, Primary (blue) and Garden (black) Candy Color Sets

ALSO
6 in. Lollipop Sticks, Parchment Triangles, Parchment Paper

INSTRUCTIONS
Bake and cool cake pops following pan instructions. Insert sticks following recipe; chill. Place on cooling grid over parchment-covered cookie sheet; cover head with melted candy. Tap to settle; chill until firm. Pipe in uniform using melted candy in cut parchment bag; tap to settle and chill to set after piping each section. Pipe in shoes, dot eyes and smile; chill. Pipe in football; chill. Pipe dot nose and hands; chill. Pipe face mask, helmet detail and laces; chill.

*Combine orange candy with a little white for skin tone shown.

e tee 'em up!

PAN
9 x 13 x 2 in. Sheet

COLORS
Red-Red, Royal Blue, Lemon Yellow

FONDANT
White Ready-To-Use Rolled Fondant (1½ oz. per treat), 10 Pc. Fondant/Gum Paste Tool Set, 9 in. Rolling Pin, Roll & Cut Mat, Brush Set

RECIPE
Favorite Cake Ball Pops, p. 7

ALSO
White Candy Dips, 8 in. Lollipop Sticks, Pops Decorating Stand; knife, ruler

INSTRUCTIONS
Prepare medium cake balls and insert sticks following recipe. Chill. Dip in melted candy. Place in Decorating Stand until set. Roll out fondant ⅛ in. thick. Cut a 5 in. circle to cover balls. Use small end of dogbone tool to imprint dimples. Tint fondant red, blue and yellow (¾ in. ball per pop). Shape 2 in. long tee with ¾ in. wide cupped top. Brush bottom of golf ball with damp brush. Slide tee up stick and attach to golf ball. Use fingers to shape and taper tee. Trim tee to 1¾ in. long.

f soccer sensations

PANS
9 x 13 x 2 in. Sheet, Silicone Boy Mold, Cooling Grid

COLORS*
Red-Red, Christmas Red, Black

FONDANT
White Ready-To-Use Rolled Fondant (½ oz. per treat), 9 in. Rolling Pin, Roll & Cut Mat, Round Cut-Outs, Brush Set

CANDY
White, Light Cocoa Candy Melts; Primary (orange, yellow) and Garden (black, violet) Candy Color Sets

RECIPE
Favorite Cake Ball Pops, p. 7

ALSO
6 in. Lollipop Sticks, 9 in. Angled Spatula, Fine Tip Primary Colors FoodWriter Edible Color Markers (black), Piping Gel, Parchment Paper, Parchment Triangles; knife

INSTRUCTIONS
Prepare cake ball mixture; press firmly into mold cavities. Chill and remove. Ice back with melted candy; chill. Set on cooling grid over parchment-covered pan; pour on melted candy tinted to desired skin tone. Tint portions of fondant red and black. Roll out fondant ⅛ in. thick. Cut 2 x ½ in. strips for shirt and shorts and a ½ in. circle for shoes; attach with Piping Gel, trimming to fit. Cut and attach ¼ in. wide collar strip, ⅛ in. wide strips for belt, neckband, stripe trim on shirt, shorts and shoes. Using melted candy in cut parchment bag, pipe dot and outline facial features, pull-out hair and hair bands; chill until firm. For soccer ball, roll out fondant ¼ in. thick; cut circle using smallest Cut-Out. Draw ball details with black FoodWriter. Attach ball to treat. Cut small opening in bottom and insert stick, securing with melted candy; chill.

*Combine Red-Red with Christmas Red for red shown.

Wilt

a) see-worthy treats

PANS
...x 13 x 2 in. Sheet, Cookie Sheet, Cooling
...rid

COLORS*
...ed-Red, Christmas Red, Lemon Yellow,
...olden Yellow, Orange, Brown, Copper
...or skin tone shown), Black

FONDANT
...White Ready-To-Use Rolled Fondant (4 oz.
...r 3 pops), 9 in. Rolling Pin, Roll & Cut
...at, Brush Set, Gum-Tex

CANDY
...hite, Light Cocoa Candy Melts, Primary
...range, red, yellow) Candy Color Sets

RECIPES
...vorite Cake Ball Pops, Buttercream Icing,
...7

ALSO
...ps Decorating Stand, 8 in. Lollipop Sticks,
...rchment Triangles, Parchment Paper;
...sposable Decorating Bags, ruler, spatula

INSTRUCTIONS
In advance: Prepare fondant pieces. Tint 1 oz. in desired skin tone. Roll 3 heads, ⅝ in. diameter. Attach tiny ball nose using damp brush. Use buttercream to pipe tip 1 dot eyes, outline smile and pull-out dot hair. Add ⅛ teaspoon Gum-Tex to 3 oz. fondant. Roll-out 1 oz. white ⅛ in. thick. Cut two 1 x 1¾ in. high sails for each boat. Divide remaining 2 oz. fondant and tint orange, red and yellow. Roll out ⅛ in. thick. Cut ½ x ⅞ in. wide pennants. Let all pieces dry overnight. Reserve remaining tinted fondant.

Prepare large cake balls. Cut in half and shape into oval boats. Chill. Tint portions of melted white candy yellow, red and orange; reserve small amount of white. Spread candy over flat side of boats; let dry flat side down on parchment paper. Set flat side down on cooling grid over parchment-covered cookie sheet. Cover with candy using cut disposable bag; tap to settle then chill until set. Pipe a line of candy around stick, 4½ in. from top; this will create a shelf to rest boat. Chill until firm, then repeat. Use knife tip to poke holes through candy shell; slide boat onto stick. Attach sails and pennant with white melted candy. Roll out reserved fondant colors ⅛ in. thick. Cut a ¼ x 7 in. strip for boat railing. Attach railing and head with melted candy.

*Combine Red-Red with Christmas Red for red fondant shown. Combine Lemon Yellow with Golden Yellow for yellow fondant shown.

b) poppin' past the planets

PANS
9 x 13 x 2 in. Sheet, Cookie Sheet, Cooling Grid

COLORS*
Orange, Violet, Rose, Brown, Red-Red, Copper (for skin tone shown)

FONDANT
White Ready-To-Use Rolled Fondant (2½ oz. per treat), 9 in. Rolling Pin, Roll & Cut Mat, Brush Set, Leaf, Oval Cut-Outs, Gum-Tex

CANDY
White Candy Melts, Garden (green), Primary (yellow) Candy Color Sets

RECIPE
Favorite crisped rice cereal treats

ALSO
Football Colored Metal Cutter Set, Primary (red, black) Fine Tip FoodWriter Edible Color Markers, 6 in. Lollipop Sticks, Parchment Triangles, Parchment Paper; knife, ruler

INSTRUCTIONS
In advance: Prepare fondant trims. Knead ¼ teaspoon Gum-Tex into each 2 oz. fondant. Tint fondant; roll out ¹⁄₁₆ in. thick as needed. For head, roll a ⅞ in. diameter ball. Roll a tiny ball nose and flattened white disks for eyes; attach using damp brush. Cut ⅜ in. triangles for hair; attach and curl up points. For tail fin, cut a violet oval using largest Cut-Out. Cut ¾ in. wide section from end; cut ¼ in. notch using football cutter. For nose trim, cut ¾ in. wide section using pointed end of football cutter. For wing, cut oval using medium Cut-Out. Use knife to cut straight edge 1 in. in from end; use football cutter to cut away curved back. Cut flames using smallest leaf cutter from set. Cut ¼ in. wide rocket tip using football cutter; attach to nose trim with damp brush. Let all pieces dry overnight.

Prepare cereal treats and press into pan, 1 in. thick. Cut rocket using football cutter from set. Melt candy. Ice bottom with melted candy; chill until firm. Position on cooling grid over parchment-covered cookie sheet. Pour on melted candy to cover. Tap to settle; chill until firm. Cut small opening for stick and attach with melted candy. Using melted candy in cut parchment bags, pipe dots and attach fondant trims. Use FoodWriter Markers to add red flame details, black dot eyes and smile.

*Combine Violet with Rose for violet shown. Combine Brown with Red-Red for brown shown. Tint white candy with green and yellow candy colors for green shown.

c) stick shifts

PAN
...x 13 x 2 in. Sheet

COLORS*
...ristmas Red, Lemon Yellow, Golden Yellow,
...ack

FONDANT
...hite Ready-To-Use Rolled Fondant (1 oz. per
...at), 9 in. Rolling Pin, Brush Set

CANDY*
...d, White Candy Melts, Primary (blue, yellow),
...rden (black, green) Candy Color Sets, Chocolate
...o Melting Pot

RECIPE
...vorite Cake Ball Pops, p. 7

ALSO
...ps Decorating Stand, 6 in. Lollipop Sticks,
...rchment Triangles; knife, ruler

INSTRUCTIONS
Prepare large cake balls; cut off bottom ⅓ to shape car. Insert sticks following recipe. Chill. Dip in melted tinted candy. Place in Decorating Stand; chill until firm. Tint fondant red, yellow, gray and black. Roll out white ¹⁄₁₆ in. thick. Cut a 1½ in. diameter circle. Cut into 4 sections for side windows. Cut ¾ x 1 in. wide strips for front and back windshields. Attach windows using damp brush. For tires, roll ½ in. diameter balls; flatten slightly. For hubcaps, roll a flat ¼ in. diameter disk. For front and back lights, roll ¼ in. diameter balls; flatten slightly. Use melted candy in cut parchment bag to attach fondant trims and pipe outline steering wheel.

*Combine Lemon Yellow with Golden Yellow for yellow fondant shown. Tint white candy with green and a little yellow candy color for green candy shown.

d) cake pop express

PANS
10.5 x 15.5 x 1 in. Jelly Roll, Cookie Sheet, Cooling Grid

TIPS
2A, 16

COLOR
Black

FONDANT
White Ready-To-Use Rolled Fondant (1 oz. per treat), 9 in. Rolling Pin, Roll & Cut Mat, Brush Set, Square Cut-Outs

CANDY*
Red, Blue, Orange, Green, Yellow, White Candy Melts, Primary (blue) Candy Color Set, Chocolate Pro Melting Pot

ALSO
Jumbo Nonpareils, Flowerful Medley (confetti), Rainbow Jimmies Sprinkles, Cake Leveler, Pops Decorating Stand, 6 in. Lollipop Sticks, Parchment Paper, Parchment Triangles; large spice drop, knife, ruler

INSTRUCTIONS
Bake and cool cake using firm-textured batter such as pound cake. Level to 1 in. high. Cut 1 large and 3 medium squares using Cut-Outs. Use knife to trim 1 in. square off engine. Dip end of stick in melted candy; push into pops. Chill. Dip in melted candy. Place in Decorating Stand; chill until firm. Dip top ¼ in. in yellow candy; let set. Pipe mound of candy over train cars; attach sprinkles. For window, set smallest square Cut-Out on parchment paper. Fill to ⅛ in. deep with white candy. Chill until set, then unmold and attach. Tint fondant black and roll out ⅛ in. thick. Cut 1 large wheel using wide end of tip 2A; cut 7 small wheels using wide end of tip 16. Cut top of spice drop flat. Use melted candy in cut parchment bags to pipe spokes and window border and to attach spice drop and wheels.

*Add blue candy color to Blue Candy Melts for blue shown.

bright smiling faces

PAN
9 x 13 x 2 in. Sheet

CANDY
White Candy Melts, Garden (black), Primary (red, yellow, blue) Candy Color Sets, Candy Eyeballs, Chocolate Pro Melting Pot

RECIPE
Favorite Cake Ball Pops, p. 7

ALSO
People Pops Sprinkle Set, Pops Decorating Stand, 6 in. Lollipop Treat Sticks, Parchment Triangles; knife, ruler

INSTRUCTIONS
Prepare small cake balls and insert sticks following recipe. Chill. Dip in melted candy. Place in Decorating Stand; chill until firm. Use tinted candy in cut parchment bag to pipe noses and to attach candy eyes, people sprinkle ears, earrings and hair. Tint candy black to pipe outline mouths.

pack of pirates

PAN
9 x 13 x 2 in. Sheet

TIP
8

COLORS
Kelly Green, Christmas Red, Royal Blue

FONDANT
White Ready-To-Use Rolled Fondant (1 oz. per treat), 9 in. Rolling Pin, Roll & Cut Mat, Brush Set, Cutter/Embosser

CANDY*
White, Red, Orange, Light Cocoa Candy Melts, Garden (black) Candy Color Set, Chocolate Pro Melting Pot

RECIPE
Favorite Cake Ball Pops, p. 7

ALSO
Pops Decorating Stand, 6 in. Cookie Treat Sticks, Parchment Triangles; knife, ruler

INSTRUCTIONS
Prepare medium cake balls and insert sticks following recipe. Chill. Dip in melted, tinted candy. Place in Decorating Stand; chill until firm. Use melted, tinted candy in cut parchment bags to pipe patch, ball nose and outline mouth; let set. For bandanas, tint fondant and roll out ¹⁄₁₆ in. thick. Cut 4 in. diameter circle; cut in half. Wrap around and attach to pop using damp brush; smooth excess to one side. Pinch and slit for ties; roll and attach small ball for knot. For dots, roll out white fondant ¹⁄₁₆ in. thick. Cut using narrow end of tip 8. Attach to bandana and eyes using damp brush. Use melted candy to pipe dot pupil and patch string.

*Tint melted light cocoa candy with red, white candy with orange or light cocoa for various skin tones shown.

c galactic goofball

PAN
9 x 13 x 2 in. Sheet

COLORS*
Violet, Rose, Orange, Christmas Red, Black

FONDANT
White Ready-To-Use Rolled Fondant (1 oz. per treat), 9 in. Rolling Pin, Roll & Cut Mat, Brush Set

CANDY
Yellow Candy Melts, Candy Eyeballs, Chocolate Pro Melting Pot

RECIPE
Favorite Cake Ball Pops, p. 7

ALSO
Pops Decorating Stand, 11¾ in. Lollipop Sticks, 4 in. Lollipop Sticks, Flowerful Medley (Confetti) Sprinkles, Parchment Triangles; black shoestring licorice, knife, ruler

INSTRUCTIONS
In advance: Make fondant trims. For hands, roll ⅜ in. balls. Flatten and cut slits for fingers. Insert 1 in. piece of licorice. For body, roll a ⅝ x ¾ in. high cylinder. Use knife to score waistline. Use toothpick to poke holes for arms. Dip end of arms in melted candy and insert. Let dry flat.

Prepare cake balls (1 large and 1 small for each pop) and insert 4 in. lollipop sticks following recipe. Chill. Dip in melted candy. Place in Decorating Stand; chill until firm. Twist to remove sticks. On 11¾ in. sticks, pipe a ring of candy around stick, 4 in. from top; this will create a shelf to rest body. Chill until firm, then repeat. Slide large pop onto stick, leaving 2½ in. extended at top; secure with melted candy. Slide on fondant body and small pop. Roll ⅜ in. fondant ball for antenna and push onto top of stick. Secure antenna and attach details using melted candy. For feet, roll ½ in. fondant balls. Shape then attach. Attach confetti ears and buttons. Roll out small amount of red and black fondant ¹⁄₁₆ in. thick. Cut out mouth and tongue; attach. Attach eyes. Pipe dot nose.

*Combine Violet with Rose for violet shown.

d cute crawlers

PAN
9 x 13 x 2 in. Sheet

CANDY
White Candy Melts, Primary (blue, orange, yellow), Garden (green, black) Candy Color Sets, Chocolate Pro Melting Pot

RECIPE
Favorite Cake Ball Pops, p. 7

ALSO
Animal Pops Sprinkle Set, Pops Decorating Stand, 8 in. Lollipop Sticks, Parchment Triangles; knife, ruler

INSTRUCTIONS
Prepare small cake balls and insert sticks following recipe. Chill. Dip in melted tinted candy. Place in Decorating Stand; chill until firm. Use tinted candy in cut parchment bag to pipe eyes, pupils and to attach animal sprinkle features. Pipe smiles, stripes and spots with tinted candy.

e stick-o-saurus

PANS
9 x 13 x 2 in. Sheet, Cookie Sheet, Cooling Grid

COLORS
Orange, Leaf Green

FONDANT
White Ready-To-Use Rolled Fondant (1½ oz. per treat), 9 in. Rolling Pin, Roll & Cut Mat, Brush Set, Gum-Tex

CANDY*
Orange, White Candy Melts, Garden (black, green), Primary (orange, yellow) Candy Color Set, Candy Eyeballs

RECIPE
Favorite Cake Ball Pops, p. 7

ALSO
Pops Treat Sticks, Parchment Triangles, Cake Boards, Parchment Paper; knife, ruler

INSTRUCTIONS
In advance: Make fondant trims. Tint fondant green and orange. Roll out green ⅛ in. thick. Cut ¼ x ⅜ in. high triangles for spikes. Add ⅛ teaspoon Gum-Tex to a ⅞ in. ball of orange; shape into 1½ x ½ in. curved head and neck. Shape a ¾ in. ball into a 1 in. long tapered tail. Let pieces dry on parchment paper-covered surface. **Also:** Make candy spots. Using green candy in a cut parchment bag, pipe ⅜ in. spots on parchment paper. Chill until set.

Prepare large cake balls and cut in half. Chill. Ice bottoms with melted candy. Place on parchment-covered cookie sheet; chill until firm. Set on cooling grid over parchment-covered cookie sheet. Pour on melted, tinted candy to cover. Tap to settle, chill until firm. Cut opening in bottom for stick; attach with melted candy. Use melted candy in cut parchment bags to attach head, tail, spikes and candy eyes. Pipe nose and smile. Attach candy spots.

*Add orange candy color to orange candy for orange shown. Tint white candy with green and yellow candy color for green spots shown.

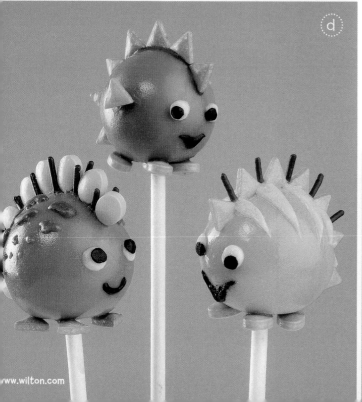

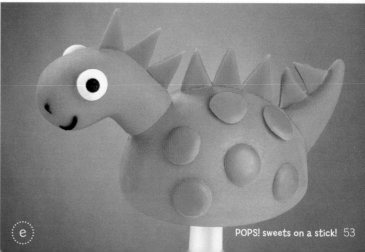

ⓐ tense trio

PANS
Silicone Round Brownie Pops Mold; Cookie Sheet, Cooling Grid

FONDANT
White Ready-To-Use Rolled Fondant (1¼ oz. per treat) Primary, Natural, Neon Fondant Multi Packs; 9 in. Rolling Pin, Roll & Cut Mat, Brush Set

CANDY*
Lavender, Orange, Yellow Candy Melts; Garden (violet) Candy Color Set

ALSO
Pops Decorating Stand, 9 in. Spatula, Parchment Paper; knife, cornstarch, black shoestring licorice, ruler

INSTRUCTIONS
Bake and cool brownie pops in silicone mold supported by cookie sheet. Ice bottom with melted candy; chill until firm. Place brownie on cooling grid over parchment-covered cookie sheet. Cover with melted candy; tap to settle. Chill. Cut a small hole in bottom and insert stick, securing with candy. Position in Decorating Stand; chill until firm. Flatten balls of white fondant and shape 1 x ¾ in. eyes; attach with damp brush. Flatten red balls into ¾ x ½ in. nose; attach. Roll small black pupils; attach. Roll out black fondant ¹⁄₁₆ in. thick; cut 1 x 5 in. long strips for hair. Cut slits ½ in. deep; roll up and secure base with water. Trim excess off bottom and attach to pops with damp brush. Fan out to shape hair. For feet, roll 1 in. fondant balls and cut in half. Cut black shoestring licorice into 1½ in. pieces; insert in feet. Cut small holes in bottom of brownie and insert legs, securing with candy. Chill to set.

*Add violet candy color to lavender candy for violet shade shown.

ⓑ hold for a hug!

PANS
3-D Mini Bear

CANDY*
White, Yellow, Orange Candy Melts; Garden (green, black) Candy Color Set, Candy Eyeballs, Chocolate Pro Melting Pot

ALSO
6 in. Lollipop Sticks, Animal Pops Sprinkles, Chocolate Jimmies, Parchment Triangles, Cake Board, 9 in. Rolling Pin, Pops Decorating Stand, Parchment Paper; spice drops, black shoestring licorice, granulated sugar, scissors, ruler, waxed paper

INSTRUCTIONS
In advance: Make foot pads. Using melted candy in cut parchment bag, pipe ½ in. ovals on parchment-covered board. Chill until firm.

Bake and cool bear cakes according to package direction. Cut off ears and trim down sides of arms. Insert sticks following Cake Ball Pops directions (p. 7); chill firm. Dip pops in green or yellow candy. Place in Decorating Stand; chill until firm. Attach feet with melted candy; ch For green monster, pipe tummy, toes, mouth and nose with melted candy; chill. Attach oval sprinkle foot pads and candy eyeballs; chill. For yellow monster, pipe cand stripes across body. For all horns, cut yellow oval sprink in half; cut horn shape and attach with candy; chill. Atta chocolate jimmies for hair and eyelashes with melted candy; chill. For green hands, roll out spice drops on waxed paper sprinkled with sugar; cut hands with scissors. Use oval sprinkles for yellow hands. Attach han to ¾ in. length of licorice with candy; chill. Cut a hole fo an arm and insert in treats.

*Combine melted white candy with green candy color and a little melted yellow candy fo green shown.

The celebration has to be a success when kids can experience a close encounter with an alien life form! While their bright candy details give them a strange, other-worldly glow, these space creatures greet all earthlings with open arms.

ⓒ try trifocals!

PANS
9 x 13 x 2 in. Sheet, Cooling Grid

CANDY
White, Red, Orange, Green Candy Melts; Garden (black) Candy Color Set, Chocolate Pro Melting Pot, Candy Eyeballs

RECIPE
Favorite Cake Ball Pops, p. 7

ALSO
Parchment Triangles, 6 in. Cookie Treat Sticks, Pops Decorating Stand; knife, spice drops, banana-shaped hard candies, craft foam block

INSTRUCTIONS
Prepare medium cake balls. Insert sticks following recipe. Chill. Dip in melted candy. Place in Decorating Stand; chill until firm. Cut small holes for ears with knife. Insert banana candies; secure with melted candy. Cut small piece of spice drop and shape for nose. Attach nose and eyes with melted candy. Using black tinted candy, pipe outline smiles; let set. Pipe dot teeth.

(d) eyes multiply!

PAN
9 x 13 x 2 in. Sheet

TIP
1

CANDY
White Candy Melts, Garden (green, violet, black), Primary (yellow, orange, blue) Candy Color Sets, Chocolate Pro Melting Pot, Candy Eyeballs

RECIPES
Favorite Cake Ball Pops, Buttercream Icing, p. 7

ALSO
Pops Decorating Stand, 6 in. Lollipop Sticks; knife, ruler

INSTRUCTIONS
Prepare small cake balls and insert sticks following recipe. Chill. Dip in melted candy. Place in Decorating Stand until set. Attach eyes and decorate using tip 1 and buttercream icing. Pipe outline or fill-in mouths and eyebrows; pipe pull-out or fill-in teeth.

(e) curly chorus

PAN
9 x 13 x 2 in. Sheet

TIP
2

COLORS
Rose, Black

FONDANT
Primary (red, yellow), Neon (orange, yellow) Colors Fondant Multi Pack (½ oz. per treat), 9 in. Rolling Pin, Brush Set

CANDY
Yellow, Blue Candy Melts, Chocolate Pro Melting Pot, Candy Eyeballs

RECIPES
Favorite Cake Ball Pops, Buttercream Icing, p. 7

ALSO
Pops Decorating Stand, 8 in. Cookie Treat Sticks, 4 in. Lollipop Sticks, Parchment Triangles, Gum-Tex; colored pipe cleaners (6 in. lengths), knife, ruler

INSTRUCTIONS
In advance: Make curls. Add ¼ teaspoon Gum-Tex to red and yellow fondant; roll out ¹⁄₁₆ in. thick. Cut ¼ in. wide strips in lengths from 1½ to 3 in. Wrap around 4 in. lollipop sticks; let set 10 to 15 minutes. Slide off and let dry overnight.

Prepare large cake balls and insert sticks following recipe. Chill. Dip in melted candy. Place in Decorating Stand; chill until firm. Attach eyes and pipe features using buttercream icing and tip 2. Outline and fill-in mouths; pat smooth. Pipe outline brows, dot cheeks (flatten slightly) and bead heart tongue. Pipe dot nose and attach curls using melted candy in cut parchment bag. Wrap pipe cleaner around stick and shape hands.

family tree treats

PANS
Silicone Boy Mold, Cookie Sheet, Cooling Grid

COLORS*
Lemon Yellow, Golden Yellow, Black, Royal Blue, Brown, Violet, Rose, Black, Leaf Green, Christmas Red, Red-Red, Orange

FONDANT
White Ready-To-Use Rolled Fondant (½ oz. per treat); 9 in. Rolling Pin; Roll & Cut Mat; Brush Set

CANDY
White, Light Cocoa Candy Melts; Garden (pink, black, violet) and Primary (green, blue, yellow, orange) Candy Color Sets

RECIPE
Pound Cake from a Cake Mix, p. 7

ALSO
6 in., 8 in. Lollipop Sticks; Pops Decorating Stand, Pops Display Stand, Parchment Paper, Parchment Triangles; knife, construction paper, scissors, markers, curling ribbon, tape

INSTRUCTIONS
Bake and cool cakes in silicone mold supported by cookie sheet. Insert sticks following Cake Ball Pops instructions (p. 7); chill until firm. Set treats on cooling grid over parchment-covered cookie sheet; cover with melted tinted candy. Chill until firm. Roll out tinted fondant ⅛ in. thick. Cut clothing to fit treats, attaching with damp brush. Pipe clothing details, facial features and hair using melted candy in cut parchment bag; chill. Cut strips of construction paper and tape to sides of stand. Print names and add dots with markers. Position pops and curling ribbon. For topper print message on paper, cut a 3½ in. circle and tape to an 8 in. stick. Add dots with markers.

*Combine Lemon Yellow with Golden Yellow for yellow shown. Combine Violet with Rose for violet shown. Combine Christmas Red with Red- Red for red shown. Tint white candy with orange candy color for light skin tone shown.

punky pops

PAN
9 x 13 x 2 in. Sheet

CANDY*
White, Green Candy Melts, Primary (orange, yellow), Garden (pink, black) Candy Color Sets, Chocolate Pro Melting Pot

RECIPE
Favorite Cake Ball Pops, p. 7

ALSO
People Pops Sprinkle Set, Pops Decorating Stand, 6 in. Lollipop Sticks, Parchment Triangles

INSTRUCTIONS
Prepare small cake balls and insert sticks following recipe. Chill. Dip in melted, tinted candy. Place in Decorating Stand; chill until firm. Use tinted candy in cut parchment bag to pipe noses and to attach icing eyes and people sprinkle hair and cheeks. Tint candy black to pipe eyes and smiles.

*Add yellow candy color to green candy for green shown.

PAN
9 x 13 x 2 in. Sheet

CANDY*
White, Orange Candy Melts; Chocolate Pro Melting Pot

RECIPE
Favorite Cake Ball Pops, p. 7

ALSO
8 in. Lollipop Sticks, People Make-A-Face Icing Decorations, Pops Decorating Stand, Parchment Triangles

INSTRUCTIONS
Prepare small cake balls and insert sticks following recipe instructions. Dip pops into melted candy; tap to settle. Place in decorating stand; chill until firm. Attach icing decoration facial features and hair with melted candy in cut parchment bag. Pipe noses with melted candy.

*Combine White with Orange Candy Melts for light skin tone shown.

The Smith Family

Wilton

d) Paws for a Treat

PAN
Cookie Sheet, Cooling Grid

CANDY*
White, Light Cocoa, Orange, Candy Melts,
Primary (blue, yellow) Candy Color Set

RECIPE
Roll-Out Cookies, p. 7

ALSO
8 in. Lollipop Sticks, Animal
Make-A-Face Icing Decorations,
Parchment Triangles, Parchment Paper,
Pops Decorating Stand, Round Cut-Outs
(large and medium used)

INSTRUCTIONS
Prepare and roll out dough. For each
animal, use large Cut-Out to cut body and
medium Cut-Out to cut head; Bake and
cool. Position cookies on cooling grid over
parchment-covered sheet. Cover with
candy. Tap to settle; chill until set. Pipe
paws with melted candy in cut parchment
bag; chill. Pipe paw pads and tiger stripes;
chill. Attach icing decoration facial features
with melted candy; chill. Attach sticks to
backs of pops with melted candy; chill.

*Add a little White Candy Melts to Light Cocoa for lighter brown shown.

ⓐ everybody in the pool!

PANS
9 x 13 x 2 in. Sheet, Silicone Boy Mold, Cookie Sheet, Cooling Grid

CANDY
White, Light Cocoa, Orange, Yellow, Red, Blue, Green Candy Melts, Garden (black, pink) Candy Color Set

RECIPE
Favorite Cake Ball Pops, p. 7

ALSO
Pops Decorating Stand, 6 in. Cookie Treat Sticks, Parchment Triangles, Parchment Paper; 3 x 8 in. diameter craft foam circle, blue curling ribbon, blue, white construction paper, scissors, knife, ruler, glue stick, tape

INSTRUCTIONS
Prepare cake ball mixture and press into silicone mold. Chill then unmold. Insert sticks following recipe. Chill. Place on cooling grid over parchment-covered cookie sheet. Pour on melted candy tinted in desired skin tone. Tap to settle; chill until firm. Use melted candy in cut parchment bags to pipe bathing suits and swim trunks, facial features and assorted hair-styles. Make pool. Cover top and wrap outside of craft foam circle with blue construction paper. Add six ¾ in. wide vertical stripes and ½ in. top border. Insert people; trimming sticks as needed. Curl 24 in. lengths of ribbon and position for water.

ⓑ mini martinis

PAN
10.5 x 15.5 x 1 in. Jelly Roll, Cookie Sheet, Cooling Grid

COLORS
Rose, Leaf Green

CANDY
White Candy Melts

ALSO
Pink, Light Green Colored Sugars, Square Cut-Outs, 8 in. Lollipop Sticks, Brush Set, Piping Gel, Parchment Paper; knife, ruler

INSTRUCTIONS
Bake and cool 1 in. high cake using firm-textured batter such as pound cake. Cut squares using largest Cut-Out. Cut diagonally to shape glass. Ice back with melted candy; chill until set. Place iced side down on cooling grid over parchment-covered board. Cover with melted candy; let set. Repeat for smooth surface. Use knife tip to poke hole in Candy Melts wafer. Slide onto stick; secure in place 1½ in. from top using melted candy. Poke hole in bottom of cake. Slide onto stick, secure with melted candy. Brush bottom half with rose and green tinted piping gel. Sprinkle on colored sugars.

Pool your pops into the splashiest centerpiece of all! Make the swimmers in the Silicone Boys Mold, add the personalized candy features and swimsuit, then display in a ribbon-topped craft block and watch the kids dive in.

c sun pops

PAN
...x 13 x 2 in. Sheet

...NDANT
...on (pink, orange), Natural (black) Fondant Multi
...cks (½ oz. per treat), 9 in. Rolling Pin, Roll & Cut Mat,
...ush Set

...NDY
...ndy Eyeballs, Yellow Candy Melts, Chocolate Pro
...lting Pot

...CIPE
...vorite Cake Ball Pops, p. 7

...SO
...n. Lollipop Sticks; Orange, Pink Colored Sugars,
...ps Decorating Stand, Parchment Triangles, Piping
...l; ruler, knife
...w.wilton.com

INSTRUCTIONS
Prepare large cake balls and insert sticks following recipe. Chill. Dip in melted candy. Place in Decorating Stand; chill until firm. For rays, roll out orange fondant ⅛ in. thick. Cut ¾ x ½ in. wide triangles; let dry. Attach to pop with melted candy. Brush rays with Piping Gel and sprinkle on orange sugar. Roll out black fondant ⅛ in. thick. Cut 1¾ x ⅝ in. base for sunglasses. Roll thin pink fondant log and attach for frames; brush with Piping Gel and sprinkle with pink sugar. Attach to ball with melted candy. Roll and attach thin logs for closed eyes. Attach Candy Eyeballs. Cut smiles; attach with damp brush. Pipe ball noses.

d flamingo flock

PAN
9 x 13 x 2 in. Sheet

COLORS*
Pink, Rose, Orange, Black

FONDANT
White Ready-To-Use Rolled Fondant (¾ oz. per treat), 9 in. Rolling Pin, Roll & Cut Mat, Brush Set

CANDY
White Candy Melts, Primary (orange), Garden (pink, black) Candy Color Sets, Chocolate Pro Melting Pot

RECIPE
Favorite Cake Ball Pops, p. 7

ALSO
Pops Decorating Stand, 8 in. Lollipop Sticks, Gum-Tex; scissors, ruler

INSTRUCTIONS
In advance: Tint small amount of fondant black and ½ oz. per pop pink; add a little Gum-Tex to pink. Shape head and neck from 2 x ½ in. log. Shape ½ in. long beak and tiny ball eyes; attach using damp brush. Let dry 24 hours. Reserve excess pink.

Prepare small cake balls and insert sticks following recipe. Chill. Dip ball and 1½ in. of stick in melted candy tinted pink. Place in Decorating Stand; chill until firm. Attach neck with melted candy; hold until set. Flatten ½ in. ball of fondant for feet. Cut slit and slide onto stick; secure with melted candy. Shape and cut slits for toes. Flatten ¾ in. balls for wings. Cut and shape. Attach using damp brush.

Combine Pink with Rose and Orange for pink fondant shown. Combine pink and orange candy colors with melted white candy for pink candy shown.

Ice cream and cake have never been so much fun! Shape the cake pops recipe in our Cordial Cups mold, add a cake ball scoop, and create the tutti-frutti colors with melted candy.

(a) Go Berry Picking

PAN
10.5 x 15.5 x 1 in. Jelly Roll

COLOR
Leaf Green

FONDANT
White Ready-To-Use Rolled Fondant (¼ oz. per treat), 9 in. Rolling Pin, Roll & Cut Mat, Brush Set, Heart, Leaf Cut-Outs

CANDY
Red, Light Cocoa, Yellow Candy Melts, Chocolate Pro Melting Pot

RECIPE
Pound Cake from a Cake Mix, p. 7

ALSO
Cake Boards, 6 in. Cookie Treat Sticks, Parchment Triangles, Parchment Paper; knife, ruler

INSTRUCTIONS
Bake and cool cake. Level to 1 in. high. Cut hearts using largest Cut-Out. Dip stick in melted candy and push into top. Chill. Dip in melted red candy; set on side on parchment-covered board. Chill. Dip bottom ⅓ in light cocoa candy; set on parchment-covered board and chill until set. Use melted yellow candy in cut parchment bag to pipe seeds; let set. Tint fondant and roll out ¹⁄₁₆ in. thick. Use smallest cutter to cut 5 leaves for each berry. Attach using damp brush. Roll ⅛ x ⅜ in. long log for stem; attach around stick using melted candy.

(b) single scoops

PANS
9 x 13 x 2 in. Sheet, Cookie Sheet, Cooling Grid

CANDY
White, Peanut Butter Candy Melts, Primary (yellow), Garden (pink, green) Candy Color Sets, Cordial Cups Candy Mold

RECIPE
Favorite Cake Ball Pops, p. 7

ALSO
Pops Treat Sticks, Parchment Triangles, Parchment Paper; knife, plastic food wrap

INSTRUCTIONS
Prepare cake ball mixture. Line Cordial Cup mold cavities with square of plastic wrap. Press in pop mixture, chill then unmold. Ice bottoms with melted candy (add white to peanut butter candy for tan shown). Place on parchment-covered cookie sheet; chill until firm. Set on cooling grid iced side down, over parchment-covered cookie sheet. Pour on melted candy to cover. Tap to settle; chill until firm. Pipe lines on sides using melted candy in cut parchment bag. Chill. For ice cream, roll large cake balls. Trim off ⅓ for flat bottom. Set on cooling grid over parchment-covered cookie sheet. Pour on melted, tinted candy to cover. Tap to settle; chill until firm. Attach to cone with melted candy. Add a drop of water to ¼ cup melted candy to thicken. Immediately use cut parchment bag to pipe ice cream edge. Attach to Pops Treat Stick using melted candy.

(c) summer slices

PANS
9 x 5 in. Loaf, Cookie Sheet, Cooling Grid

CANDY*
Red, White, Green Candy Melts, Garden (black) Candy Color Set

RECIPE
Pound Cake from a Cake Mix, p. 7

ALSO
Round Comfort-Grip Cutter, 6 in. Lollipop Sticks, Parchment Triangles, Cake Boards, 9 in. Angled Spatula, Parchment Paper; knife, ruler

INSTRUCTIONS
Bake and cool cake. Cut into ½ in. wide slices. Cut rounds with cutter. Cut each round into 5ths. Ice bottoms with melted red candy; chill until set. Set iced side down on cooling grid set over parchment-covered cookie sheet. Pour on red candy to cover; chill until firm on parchment-covered boards. Dip round edge in melted white candy; chill. Dip edge in melted green candy; chill. Use melted, tinted candy in cut parchment bag to pipe seeds; let set. Use knife tip to cut opening for stick. Insert stick and secure with melted candy.

*Mix equal parts of red and white candy for red candy shown. Tint small portion of green candy with black candy color to make black.

(b)

Wilt

Serve up a slice of summer with cool watermelon wedges on sticks! In this case, the seeds only add to the fun—just pipe beads of melted candy.

d easy-as-pie crispy pops

PAN
10.5 x 15.5 x 1 in. Jelly Roll

COLORS*
Ivory, Brown

FONDANT
White Ready-To-Use Rolled Fondant (½ oz. per treat); 9 in. Rolling Pin; Roll & Cut Mat; Cutter/Embosser

CANDY*
White, Red, Yellow, Peanut Butter Candy Melts; Chocolate Pro Melting Pot

RECIPE
Favorite crisped rice cereal treats

ALSO
Comfort-Grip Round Cutter; 6 in. Lollipop Sticks; Cinnamon Drops Sprinkles; Cake Board; Parchment Paper; knife, ruler

INSTRUCTIONS
Prepare cereal treats mixture and press ¾ in. high in Jelly Roll Pan. Unmold and cut circles using round cutter. Cut into 6 wedges with knife. Dip end of stick in melted candy and insert in round side of treat; chill. Dip treat in melted tan candy; chill until firm on parchment-covered board. Ice sides and top with melted red candy. Cut Cinnamon Drops in half and position for cherries. Chill.

Roll out fondant ¹⁄₁₆ in. thick. Cut lattice strips ½ to 1½ in. long x ⅛ in. wide. Attach to top with melted candy. For border, roll two ropes, 2 x ¹⁄₁₆ in. diameter. Twist together and attach with melted candy. Cut a 3½ x ⅛ in. high strip for back crust; attach with melted candy.

*Tint White Candy Melts with a few disks each of Peanut Butter and Yellow Candy Melts for tan crust color shown. Combine Ivory with Brown for tan fondant color shown.

ⓐ a new take on tacos

PANS
10.5 x 15.5 x 1 in. Jelly Roll, Cooling Grid, Cookie Sheet

COLORS
Orange, Leaf Green

CANDY
Yellow, Light Cocoa Candy Melts, Chocolate Pro Melting Pot

ALSO
Black Colored Sugar, Round Cut-Outs, 8 in. Lollipop Sticks, Parchment Paper; shredded coconut, red spice drops, knife, ruler, zip-close plastic bags

INSTRUCTIONS
Bake and cool cake using firm-textured batter such as pound cake. Level to ¾ in. high. Cut rounds using largest Cut-Out; cut in half. Mix black sugar melted yellow candy. Ice straight edge of the cake with candy; ch to set. Set candy side down on cooling grid over parchment-covered pan. Pour on candy to cover. Tap to settle; chill. Use kn tip to cut hole in bottom. Insert stick and secure with candy. In zip-close bags, tint coconut gree and orange. Use melted light cocoa candy in cut parchment b to pipe across center for meat; immediately sprinkle on tinted coconut, lettuce and cheese. Cu spice drops for tomatoes; attach with melted candy.

ⓑ pizza with pizazz

PAN
Round Pops Cookie Pan

RECIPE
Vanilla Sugar Cookies on a Stick, p. 7

CANDY
Red, White Candy Melts

ALSO
8 in. Cookie Treat Sticks, Parchment Triangles; green candied cherries (cut up), chocolate chips, knife

INSTRUCTIONS
Bake and cool cookies with sticks. Ice cookie with melted red candy for sauce. Position chips for sausage. Use melted white candy in cut parchment bag to pipe on cheese. Immediately sprinkle on cherries for peppers.

Wilt

ⓒ hand me a hamburger

PANS
9 x 13 x 2 in. Sheet, Cookie Sheet, Cooling Grid

COLORS*
Leaf Green, Orange, Lemon Yellow

FONDANT
White Ready-To-Use Rolled Fondant (¼ oz. per treat), 9 in. Rolling Pin, Roll & Cut Mat, Brush Set, Square and Round Cut-Outs

CANDY*
Red, White, Light Cocoa, Peanut Butter Candy Melts, Chocolate Pro Melting Pot

RECIPE
Chocolate Cake Ball Pops, p. 7

ALSO
Pops Decorating Stand, Pops Treat Sticks, Parchment Triangles, Parchment Paper; knife, ruler

INSTRUCTIONS
Prepare medium cake balls. For top bun, cut and use top ⅓ of ball. Press bottom ⅔ into medium round Cut-Out to shape bottom bun. Chill. Place buns on cooling rack set over cookie sheet. Cover with melted candy. Chill. For patty, shape a medium cake ball. Dip in melted candy, work candy into cake mixture and immediately flatten into ½ in. diameter patty. Chill. Use melted candy in cut parchment bag to pipe extra layer of candy over top, then bottom, to strengthen patty. Chill. Tint fondant for cheese and lettuce; roll out ¹⁄₁₆ in. thick. For lettuce, shape and crease 5-6 flat teardrop shapes, 1 in. long. For cheese, cut a square using medium Cut-Out. Stack pieces on stick, securing with melted candy. Use melted red candy in cut parchment bag to pipe ketchup.

*Combine Orange with Lemon Yellow for yellow fondant shown. Combine white and peanut butter candy for bun color shown.

ⓓ show-stopper pops

PAN
9 x 13 x 2 in. Sheet

FONDANT
White Ready-To-Use Rolled Fondant (6 oz. per box), Brush Set, Yellow Pearl Dust

RECIPE
Favorite Cake Ball Pops, p. 7

CANDY
White Candy Dips

ALSO
Popcorn Treat Boxes, Pops Decorating Stand, 8 in. Lollipop Sticks; mini marshmallows, white construction paper, thick and thin red markers, knife, ruler, double-stick tape

INSTRUCTIONS
In advance: Prepare box. Use ruler to make ⅛ in. wide red stripes, ½ in. apart. Cut a 2½ in. wide white paper circle; use markers to make red border and print name. Tape to box.

Prepare 13 irregularly-shaped cake balls, ⅞ in. diameter and insert sticks following recipe. Chill. Dip in melted candy. Place in Decorating Stand; chill until firm. Squish marshmallows (some whole, some halves) for random shapes. Use melted candy to attach to pops for popcorn shape. Chill. Dip entire pop in melted candy. Place in Decorating Stand; chill until firm. Brush on Pearl Dust highlights. Press 6 oz. fondant into bottom of box. Insert treats.

A fresh way to pop corn! Shape the pops recipe and add squished marshmallows to create each candy-covered kernel. Our Popcorn Treat Boxes create the perfect personalized container.

5-star pops

PANS
10.5 x 15.5 x 1 in. Jelly Roll, Cooling Grid

CANDY
Yellow Candy Melts, Garden (black) Candy Color Sets, Candy Eyeballs

RECIPE
Pound Cake from a Cake Mix, p. 7

ALSO
Star Plastic Nesting Cutter Set, 8 in. Cookie Treat Sticks, Cake Boards, Parchment Triangles, Parchment Paper; knife

INSTRUCTIONS
Bake and cool 1 in. high cake. Cut stars using 2nd smallest star cutter as a guide. Attach sticks following pops recipe (p. 7). Ice bottom with melted candy; chill on parchment paper. Place on cooling grid over parchment-covered pan and cover with melted candy; chill until firm. Attach candy eyes; outline and pipe in mouths with melted candy.

ⓑ grizzly grads

PAN
3-D Mini Bear

COLORS*
Red-Red, Christmas Red, Royal Blue, Leaf Green, Lemon Yellow, Golden Yellow

FONDANT
White Ready-To-Use Rolled Fondant (1 oz. per treat) 9 in. Rolling Pin, Roll & Cut Mat, Square Cut-Outs, Brush Set, Cutter/Embosser

CANDY
White, Light Cocoa Candy Melts; Garden (black) Candy Color Set

ALSO
6 in. Lollipop Sticks, Parchment Triangles, Pops Decorating Stand, Parchment Paper; knife, ruler

INSTRUCTIONS
Bake and cool bears following package directions. Insert sticks following Cake Ball Pops directions (p. 7); chill until firm. Dip pops in melted candy; tap to settle. Place in Decorating Stand; chill until firm. Using melted candy in cut parchment bag, pipe inside ears, paw pads and muzzle; chill until firm. Pipe dot eyes, nose and outline mouth with melted black candy; chill.

For diplomas, roll out fondant 1/16 in. thick. Cut 1 x 1½ in. rectangle; roll up and secure with damp brush. Shape a 1/16 in. diameter rope of red fondant into a bow; attach with damp brush. For mortarboard, flatten a ¼ in. ball of fondant for base. For top, roll out fondant ⅛ in. thick; cut a ¾ in. square. Roll a 1 in. yellow rope for tassel. Attach a ⅛ in. ball to end with damp brush and flatten with finger. Cut slits for fringe with knife. Attach tassel and a ⅛ in. flattened ball for top button to mortarboard with damp brush.

*Combine Red-Red and Christmas Red for red fondant shown. Combine Lemon Yellow and Golden Yellow for yellow fondant shown. Add a little melted white candy to cocoa candy for light brown shown. Tint melted light cocoa candy with black color for black shown.

Wilt

pop and circumstance

N
13 x 2 in. Sheet

NDANT
mary Colors (blue, red,
low) Fondant Multi Pack (1
per treat), 9 in. Rolling Pin,
l & Cut Mat, Brush Set,
m-Tex

NDY*
hite, Light Cocoa Candy
lts, Primary (orange),
den (black) Candy Color
s, Candy Eyeballs

CIPE
orite Cake Ball Pops, p. 7

SO
os Decorating Stand, 6 in.
lipop Sticks, Parchment Tri-
gles; knife, ruler, cornstarch

INSTRUCTIONS

In advance: Make fondant caps. Prepare fondant; add ¼ teaspoon Gum-Tex for each 4 oz. of fondant. Roll out red and blue ⅛ in. thick. Cut 1¼ in. squares. Let dry overnight on cornstarch-dusted surface. Reserve remaining fondant.

Prepare medium cake balls and insert sticks following recipe. Chill. Dip in melted candy. Place in Decorating Stand; chill until firm. Use melted candy in cut parchment bags to attach candy eyes and to pipe dot nose, outline smiles and various hairdos. Roll a ¾ in. fondant ball; flatten into a ⅜ in. thick disk for cap base. Attach to top of head with melted candy. Attach square. For tassel, roll out yellow fondant ¹⁄₁₆ in. thick. Cut a 1 ¼ x ¾ in. long strip. Cut very thin slits, ¾ in. deep, for fringe, leaving top ½ in. uncut. Roll up uncut section, smooth and flatten to ¾ in. long. Attach to cap using damp brush. Roll and attach a tiny ball button.

*Tint melted white candy light orange for light skin tone and add a little white candy to light cocoa candy for dark skin tone shown.

the future's wrapped up!

N
13 x 2 in. Sheet

LORS*
d-Red, Christmas Red

NDANT
hite Ready-To-Use Rolled
ndant (2½ oz. per treat), 9
Rolling Pin, Roll & Cut Mat,
ush Set

CIPE
orite Cake Ball Pops, p. 7

SO
hite Candy Melts, Plastic
wel Rods (4 in. lengths),
ps Decorating Stand, 8 in.
lipop Sticks; knife, ruler

INSTRUCTIONS

Prepare cake ball mixture and firmly pack into a 4 in. dowel rod. Insert sticks per recipe. Chill 2 hours or more. Push out of dowel rods. Dip in melted candy. Place in Decorating Stand; chill until firm. Roll out white fondant ⅛ in. thick. Cut a 4¼ x 4 in. piece and attach around pop with damp brush, leaving end loose. For ribbon, tint fondant red and roll out ⅛ in. thick. Cut a ¼ x 4 in. strip for ribbon, a ¼ x 6 in. strip to form bow loops and a ¼ x ¾ in. strip for knot. Attach using damp brush.

*Combine Red-Red with Christmas Red for red shown.

Don't wait for a party to pass out the pops! A great report card or helping out around the house are perfect reasons for a fun pops reward—like this smiling star!

w.wilton.com

pops for all seasons!

What if you could wave a magic wand that would instantly make kids smile? A decorated seasonal pop does the trick! It's the kind of up-close and personal treat that really clicks with kids! Even after children bring home their haul of Halloween candy, the ghost pop you gave them will stick in their memories. Whether it's Uncle Sam, a snowman or an Easter chick, pops put the color and fun of every season in the palm of your hand.

Wilt

a) sweet scrolls

PANS
Heart Pops Cookie Pan, Cookie Sheet, Cooling Grid

TIPS
2, 4

COLOR
Rose

RECIPES
Vanilla Sugar Cookies on a Stick, Color Flow Icing, p. 7

ALSO
Color Flow Mix, 8 in. Cookie Treat Sticks, Parchment Paper

INSTRUCTIONS
Prepare cookie dough and press into treat pan with 8 in. sticks. Bake and cool. Set cookies on cooling grid over parchment-covered cookie sheet. Cover with thinned rose icing; let dry. Use full-strength white icing to pipe tip 2 outline about ¾ in. from edge; let set. Flow in with thinned icing. Let dry. Use full-strength rose icing to pipe tip 2 scrolls and tip 4 bead border.

b) heart sparkle

PANS
Silicone Heart Pops Mold, Cookie Sheet, Cooling Grid

CANDY
White, Red Candy Melts; Garden (pink) Candy Color Set

RECIPE
Pound Cake from a Cake Mix, p. 7

ALSO
8 in. Cookie Treat Sticks, Red Colored Sugar, Parchment Triangles

INSTRUCTIONS
Bake and cool heart pops in silicone mold supported by cookie sheet. Tint melted white candy pink using candy color. Cover hearts on each pop with melted pink candy in cut parchment bag; chill until firm. Outline hearts with melted red candy in cut parchment bag; sprinkle with red sugar. Chill until firm.

Wilt

Happy heart cookie pops send your love more sweetly than any Valentine card! No cutting needed for these big, bold treats—just press cookie dough, along with a stick, into our Heart Pops Cookie Pan, bake then decorate with Color Flow Icing.

c a hearty hello

PANS
Heart Pops Cookie Pan, Cookie Sheet, Cooling Grid

TIPS
2, 4

COLORS*
Christmas Red, Red-Red, Black, Rose

RECIPES
Vanilla Sugar Cookies on a Stick, Color Flow Icing, p. 7

ALSO
Color Flow Mix, 8 in. Cookie Treat Sticks, Parchment Paper

INSTRUCTIONS
Prepare cookie dough and press into treat pan with 8 in. sticks. Bake and cool. Set cookies on cooling grid over parchment-covered cookie sheet. Pour on thinned color flow icing to cover. Tap to settle; let dry. Use full-strength icing to pipe tip 4 eyes (flatten with finger) and dot pupils, tip 2 dot nose and outline and fill in mouth or lips (smooth with fingertip). Pipe tip 2 outline lashes and mouth line. Pipe tip 4 dot cheeks (flatten with finger).

*Combine Christmas Red with Red-Red for red shown.

d happiness hearts

PANS
9 x 13 x 2 in. Sheet, Silicone Petite Heart Mold, Cookie Sheet, Cooling Grid

CANDY
Light Cocoa, White Candy Melts

RECIPE
Favorite Cake Ball Pops, p. 7

ALSO
6 in. Cookie Treat Sticks, Parchment Triangles, Angled Spatula, Parchment Paper

INSTRUCTIONS
Prepare cake ball mixture and press into silicone mold. Chill; unmold then insert sticks following recipe. Chill. Ice back side smooth with melted candy; chill until firm. Place candy side down on cooling grid over parchment-covered cookie sheet. Cover with melted candy using cut parchment bag; tap to settle then chill until set. Add a drop of water to ¼ cup of melted white candy. Working quickly, pipe heart outline using cut parchment bag; let set.

e five of hearts

PANS
Silicone Heart Pops Mold, Cookie Sheet, Cooling Grid

CANDY
White, Red Candy Melts, Garden (pink) Candy Color Set

RECIPE
Pound Cake from a Cake Mix, p. 7

ALSO
Red, Pink Colored Sugar, 8 in. Cookie Treat Sticks, Parchment Triangles

INSTRUCTIONS
Bake and cool cake pops with sticks in silicone mold supported by cookie sheet. Use melted candy in cut parchment bags to outline and fill in red hearts; sprinkle on colored sugar; chill. Outline and fill in pink hearts with tinted candy; sprinkle on sugar. Chill until firm.

a) heart heights

PANS
Silicone Round Brownie Pops Mold, Cookie Sheet, Cooling Grid

COLOR
Rose

FONDANT
White Ready-To-Use Rolled Fondant (¼ oz. per treat), 9 in. Rolling Pin, Roll & Cut Mat, Brush Set, Heart Cut-Outs, Fine Tip Primary Colors FoodWriter Edible Color Markers

ALSO
White Candy Melts, Chocolate Pro Melting Pot, Heart Pops Wraps, Pops Decorating Stand, Parchment Paper, 6 in. Cookie Treat Sticks; knife, ruler, cornstarch

INSTRUCTIONS
In advance: Prepare hearts. Tint fondant and roll out ⅛ in. thick. Cut hearts using medium Cut-Out. Let dry overnight on parchment-covered surface dusted with cornstarch.

Bake and cool brownie pops in silicone mold supported by cookie sheet. Insert sticks following pops recipe (p. 7). Chill. Dip in melted candy. Place in Decorating Stand; chill until firm. Write message on heart with red FoodWriter. Attach heart with melted candy. Slide on 2 heart wraps and secure with dot of candy.

b) pops of passion!

PANS
9 x 13 x 2 in. Sheet, Silicone Petite Heart Mold

CANDY
White Candy Melts, Primary (red), Garden (pink) Candy Colors, Chocolate Pro Melting Pot

RECIPE
Favorite Cake Ball Pops, p. 7

ALSO
6 in. Cookie Treat Sticks, Parchment Triangles, Parchment Paper

INSTRUCTIONS
Prepare cake ball mixture and press into silicone mold, chill and unmold. Dip stick in melted candy and insert in cake. Chill. Tint melted candy in pink and red. Dip cakes in candy; tap to smooth, chill until firm. Pipe message using melted candy in cut parchment bag. Let set.

c) hearts giving hugs

PANS
x 13 x 2 in. Sheet, Silicone Petite Heart Mold, Cooling Grid

COLOR
ack

FONDANT
hite Ready-To-Use Rolled Fondant (½ oz. per treat), 9 in. Rolling
n, Roll & Cut Mat, Brush Set

CANDY
ed Candy Melts, Candy Eyeballs

RECIPE
vorite Cake Ball Pops, p. 7

ALSO
in. Cookie Treat Sticks, Parchment Triangles, Disposable Decorating
ags, Parchment Paper; black shoestring licorice, knife, ruler

INSTRUCTIONS
Prepare cake ball mixture and press into mold. Chill then
unmold. Insert sticks following recipe. Ice back side smooth
with melted candy; chill until firm. Place candy side down
on cooling grid over parchment-covered cookie sheet.
Cover with melted candy using cut disposable bag; tap to
settle then chill until set. Roll ½ in. balls of white fondant for
hands. Flatten, shape and cut slits for fingers. Tint some
fondant black. Shape ½ in. balls into ½ x ¾ in. oval shoes.
Push hands and shoes onto 1¼ in. lengths of licorice. Use tip
of knife to poke holes in body; attach arms and legs with
melted candy. Use candy to pipe dot nose and attach eyes.
Roll out black fondant ¹⁄₁₆ in. thick. Cut ¾ in. wide smile and
attach with melted candy.

d) high-rise hearts

PAN
Silicone Heart Pops Mold, Cookie Sheet

CANDY*
White, Lavender Candy Melts, Primary (yellow), Garden (pink,
green) Candy Color Sets,

RECIPE
Pound Cake from a Cake Mix, p. 7

ALSO
6 in. Cookie Treat Sticks, Parchment Triangles, Cake Boards,
Parchment Paper

INSTRUCTIONS
Bake and cool heart pops in silicone mold supported by cookie
sheet. Cover top, middle and bottom hearts on each pop with
melted candy in cut parchment bags; chill until firm. Cover 2nd and
4th hearts; chill.

*Combine melted Lavender with a little White Candy Melts for light lavender shown.

a ears to you!

PANS
10.5 x 15.5 x 1 in. Jelly Roll, Cooling Grid

FONDANT
White Ready-To-Use Rolled Fondant (½ oz. per treat), 9 in. Rolling Pin, Roll & Cut Mat, Brush Set, Round, Oval Cut-Outs, Gum-Tex

CANDY
White Candy Melts, Garden (pink, black) Candy Color Set, Candy Eyeballs

RECIPE
Pound Cake from a Cake Mix, p. 7

ALSO
Pink Colored Sugar, 8 in. Cookie Treat Sticks, Parchment Triangles, Parchment Paper; knife, ruler

INSTRUCTIONS
In advance: Make ears. Add ¼ teaspoon Gum-Tex to each 3 oz. of fondant. Roll out ⅛ in. thick. Cut using largest oval Cut-Out. Move Cut-Out over and cut again for 1 ¾ x ¾ in. wide ears. Let dry overnight on parchment-covered surface.

Bake and cool cake. Level to 1 in. high. Cut rounds using largest Cut-Out. Ice bottoms of cakes with melted candy; chill to set. Set candy side down on cooling grid over parchment-covered pan. Pour on candy to cover. Tap to settle; chill. Use knife tip to cut hole in bottom. Insert stick and secure with candy. Use melted candy in cut parchment bag to pipe inner ear and dot nose; immediately sprinkle ears with pink sugar. Attach Candy Eyeballs and pipe whiskers and mouth using melted candy. Cut slit in top for ears and insert, securing with melted candy.

b jelly bean basket

PANS
9 x 13 x 2 in. Sheet, Mini Muffin

COLOR
Leaf Green

FONDANT
White Ready-To-Use Rolled Fondant (¼ oz. per treat), 9 in. Rolling Pin, Brush Set, Gum-Tex

RECIPE
Favorite Cake Ball Pops, p. 7

ALSO
White Candy Melts, Pops Treat Sticks, Cake Boards, Parchment Triangles, Parchment Paper; mini jelly beans, shredded coconut, knife, ruler, zip-close plastic bag

INSTRUCTIONS
In advance: Make fondant handle. Add Gum-Tex to fondant (¼ teaspoon per 4 oz. fondant). Roll 2 logs, ¼ x 3 in. long. Twist together and shape curve, 1¾ in. wide at base. Let dry on parchment-covered board.
Also: Tint coconut. Place a small amount of coconut in plastic bag. Add a little green icing color. Close bag and knead to tint.

Prepare cake ball mixture and press into muffin pan cavities; chill then unmold. Ice wide end with melted candy; chill. Set candy side down on cooling grid over parchment-covered cookie sheet. Pour on melted candy to cover. Tap to settle, chill until set. Attach handle with melted candy. Ice top with melted candy and sprinkle on green tinted coconut. Use melted candy to attach jelly beans. With knife tip, cut small opening in bottom of basket; attach to treat stick with melted candy.

Wilt⊙

The Easter bunny hops out of the hutch and into kids' hands! Candy-coated cakes with perked-up fondant ears are perfect place holders at the holiday brunch and are a great finishing touch for any Easter basket.

c) nesting bluebirds

PAN
x 13 x 2 in. Sheet

COLORS*
Lemon Yellow, Golden Yellow, Sky Blue, Kelly Green, Brown, Black

FONDANT
White Ready-To-Use Rolled Fondant (½ oz. per treat), 9 in. Rolling n, Brush Set

CANDY
White, Light Cocoa Candy Melts, Primary (blue) Candy Color Set, hocolate Pro Melting Pot

RECIPE
avorite Cake Ball Pops, p. 7

ALSO
ops Decorating Stand, 6 in. Cookie Treat Sticks, Parchment Triangles, ps! Treat Sticks; shredded coconut, zip-close plastic bag, knife, ruler

INSTRUCTIONS
Prepare small cake balls and insert sticks following recipe. Chill. Dip in melted tinted candy. Place in Decorating Stand until set. Remove sticks. Tint coconut brown. Place a small amount of coconut in plastic bag. Add a little brown icing color. Close bag and knead to tint. Spread melted light cocoa candy over top of Pops Treat Stick; build coconut nest. Chill. Secure cake balls in nests with melted candy. Chill. Tint fondant for trims. Roll cone-shaped beak, ¼ in. long. Use knife to indent beak opening. Roll tiny dot eyes. For wings, roll out blue ¹/₁₆ in. thick. Use knife to cut ¾ x ½ in. wings; cut v-shaped notches for feathers. Attach trims using melted candy.

*Combine Lemon Yellow with Golden Yellow for yellow shown. Combine Sky Blue with Kelly Green for blue fondant shown.

d) chipper chirpers

PAN
x 13 x 2 in. Sheet

COLORS*
range, Lemon Yellow, Golden Yellow

FONDANT
White Ready-To-Use Rolled Fondant (½ oz. per treat); 9 in. Rolling n; Roll & Cut Mat; Heart Cut-Outs

CANDY
White, Yellow Candy Melts; Garden (black) Candy Color Set, hocolate Pro Melting Pot

RECIPE
avorite Cake Ball Pops, p. 7

ALSO
n. Cookie Treat Sticks, Pops Decorating Stand, Parchment Triangles; ife

INSTRUCTIONS
Prepare small cake balls and insert stick following recipe; chill until firm. Dip pops in melted candy. Place in Decorating Stand; chill until firm. Tint 1 oz. portions of fondant orange and yellow; roll out ⅛ in. thick. Cut feet and wings using smallest heart Cut-Out. For feather on head, cut ½ in. teardrop shapes. Cut 2 slits ⅛ in. apart. For beak, cut two ⅜ x ¼ in. triangles; attach together with melted candy and chill until firm. Attach all fondant features with melted candy; chill until firm. Using black tinted candy in cut parchment bag, pipe dot eyes; let set.

*Combine Lemon Yellow and Golden Yellow for yellow fondant hown.

e) fresh eggs

PANS
ookie Sheet, Cooling Grid

CANDY*
White Candy Melts, Primary (yellow, blue), Garden (pink, green, olet) Candy Color Sets, Candy Melting Tray

RECIPE
ll-Out Cookies, p. 7

ALSO
d Cookie Cutters Set (egg), Pops Flower Pot Kit, Yellow, hite Pearl Dust; Blue, Lavender Colored Sugar; Jumbo Confetti rinkles, Imitation Clear Vanilla Extract; Brush Set; 8 in. Cookie eat Sticks; Parchment Triangles, Parchment Paper; green curling bon, lavender construction paper, scissors, glue stick

INSTRUCTIONS
Prepare and roll out dough. Cut 5 cookies using egg cutter from set. Bake and cool cookies. Set on cooling grid over parchment-covered cookie sheet. Pour on melted, tinted candy to cover. Tap to settle; chill until firm. Use melted candy in cut parchment bag to pipe spirals, stripes and to attach confetti. While still wet, sprinkle some stripes with Colored Sugar, working with one color at time. Let other stripes and swirls dry and paint with Pearl Dust/ vanilla mixture. Attach sticks to back using melted candy. Cut ½ in. strips of construction paper; glue to each section of flower pot. Insert eggs, fill with green curling ribbon.

*Tint melted white candy with Violet and Pink candy colors for violet shown. Tint melted white candy with Green and Yellow candy colors for green shown.

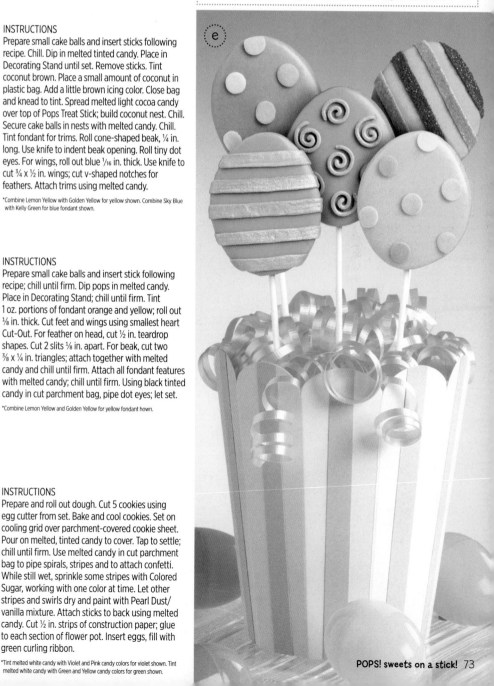

ww.wilton.com

ⓐ stars and bars

PANS
Cookie Sheet, Cooling Grid

CANDY
Red, White, Yellow Candy Melts, Primary (blue) Candy Color Set

RECIPE
Roll-Out Cookies, p. 7

ALSO
101 Cookie Cutters Set (flag), White Nonpareils, 6 in. Cookie Treat Sticks, Parchment Triangles

INSTRUCTIONS
Prepare and roll out dough. Cut cookies using flag cutter from set. Bake and co⟨⟩ Decorate using melted candy in cut parchment bags. Pipe in blue background; let set 1 minute, then sprinkle with white nonpareils. Chill until firm. Pipe alternating stripes and flagpole; chill until firm. Attach stick to back usin⟨⟩ melted candy.

ⓑ stars galore

PANS
Silicone Star Pops Mold, Cookie Sheet, Cooling Grid

CANDY
White, Red Candy Melts, Primary (blue) Candy Color Set

RECIPE
Pound Cake from a Cake Mix, p. 7

ALSO
White, Blue, Red Colored Sugar, 8 in. Cookie Treat Sticks, Parchment Triangles; knife, ruler

INSTRUCTIONS
Bake and cool cake pops with sticks in silicone mold supported by cookie sheet. Use melted candy in cut parchment bags to outline and fill in re⟨⟩ stars; sprinkle on sugar. Chill until firm. Outline and fill in blue star with tinted candy; sprinkle on sugar. Chill until firm Outline and fill in white stars with candy; sprinkle on sugar. Chill until firm

ⓒ popping fireworks

PANS
Star Cookie Pops Pan, Cookie Sheet, Cooling Grid

COLOR
Royal Blue

FONDANT
White Ready-To-Use Rolled Fondant (¼ oz. per treat), 9 in. Rolling Pin, Roll & Cut Mat, Brush Set, Star Cut-Outs

RECIPE
Vanilla Sugar Cookies on a Stick, p. 7

ALSO
White Candy Melts, Red Colored Sugar, 8 in. Cookie Treat Sticks, Parchment Triangles, Parchment Paper; white curling ribbon (12 in. per treat)

INSTRUCTIONS
Bake and cool cookies with sticks. Set ⟨⟩ cooling grid over parchment-covered cookie sheet. Cover with melted white candy; tap to settle then chill until firm on parchment-covered surface. Use melted candy in cut parchment bag to pipe stripes; immediately sprinkle on r⟨⟩ sugar. Let set. Tint fondant blue and ro⟨⟩ out ¹⁄₁₆ in. thick. Cut stars using mediu⟨⟩ Cut-Out. Attach using melted candy. T⟨⟩ ribbon around stick.

Wilt⟨⟩

d starshine sweets

PANS
Silicone Round Brownie Pops Mold, Non-Stick Cookie Sheet

ALSO
White Candy Melts, 6 in. Cookie Treat Sticks, Red, White, Blue Colored Sugars, Parchment Triangles, Star Cut-Outs, Piping Gel, Parchment Paper; craft block

INSTRUCTIONS
Bake and cool brownie pops in silicone mold supported by cookie sheet; unmold and set on parchment paper. Using melted candy in cut parchment bag, pipe around base of pop; let set 1 minute then sprinkle with sugar; chill. Dip stick in melted candy then insert into pop. Position medium star Cut-Out on cookie sheet; fill ⅛ in. thick with melted candy. Chill until firm; unmold. Brush with Piping Gel and sprinkle with sugar. Attach to pop with melted candy; chill.

e rocket pops

PAN
9 x 13 x 2 in. Sheet

COLORS*
Christmas Red, Red-Red, Royal Blue, Lemon Yellow, Golden Yellow

FONDANT
White Ready-To-Use Rolled Fondant, 9 in. Rolling Pin, Roll & Cut Mat, Brush Set, Star Cut-Outs, Gum-Tex

RECIPE
Favorite Cake Ball Pops, p. 7

ALSO
White Candy Melts, Pops Decorating Stand, 8 in. Cookie Treat Sticks, Plastic Dowel Rods (cut into 3 in. lengths), Red, Blue Colored Sugars, Chocolate Pro Melting Pot; knife, ruler

INSTRUCTIONS
In advance: Make stars. Add ¼ teaspoon Gum-Tex to 2 oz. fondant. Tint fondant and roll out ⅛ in. thick. Cut using medium star Cut-Out. Let dry.

Firmly pack 3 in. dowel rod with cake ball mixture. Insert stick per recipe, letting 1 in. extend from top end. Chill 2 hours or more. To release, push up bottom of stick through dowel rod. Dip treat in melted candy; chill until firm. Use knife to scrape candy from exposed area of stick. For each treat, tint a 1 in. ball of fondant blue or red. Roll into a log, then roll out ⅛ in. thick. Cut a ⅜ x 10 in. long strip. Attach with Candy Melts. Brush strip with water and cover with colored sugar. Attach star with melted candy.

*Combine Christmas Red with Red-Red for red shown. Combine Lemon Yellow with Golden Yellow for yellow shown.

f sam leads the parade

PAN
9 x 13 x 2 in. Sheet

TIPS
3, 46

COLORS*
Christmas Red, Red-Red, Black

CANDY*
White Candy Melts, Primary (blue, orange) Candy Color Set, Cordial Cups Candy Mold, Chocolate Pro Melting Pot

RECIPES
Favorite Cake Ball Pops, Buttercream Icing, p. 7

ALSO
Round Cut-Outs, Pops Decorating Stand, 6 in. Cookie Treat Sticks, Parchment Paper; knife, ruler

INSTRUCTIONS
In advance: Prepare candy hats. For top, fill cordial cups mold about ¾ full with melted white candy. Tap to settle; chill until firm. For brim, tint candy blue. Line pan with parchment paper. Set medium round Cut-Out on pan and fill ⅛ in. thick with melted candy. Tap to settle; chill until firm. Attach to top using melted candy.

Prepare medium cake balls and insert sticks per recipe. Chill. Dip in melted, tinted candy. Place in Decorating Stand; chill until set. Pipe tip 3 hair using buttercream icing. Attach hat using melted candy. Use icing to pipe tip 3 features and tip 46 red and white stripes.

*Combine Christmas Red with Red-Red for red shown. Tint melted white candy with orange candy color for skin tone shown.

a wolf 'em down

PAN
9 x 13 x 2 in. Sheet

COLORS
Black, Lemon Yellow

FONDANT
White Ready-To-Use Rolled Fondant (¼ oz. per treat),
9 in. Rolling Pin, Roll & Cut Mat, Brush Set

CANDY
Light Cocoa, White Candy Melts

RECIPE
Favorite Cake Ball Pops, p. 7

ALSO
Pops Decorating Stand, 6 in. Cookie Treat Sticks,
shredded coconut, knife, ruler

INSTRUCTIONS
Prepare medium cake balls and insert sticks following recipe. Chill. Dip in melted candy. Place in Decorating Stand; chill until firm. Tint a small amount of fondant yellow and black. Roll out yellow ⅛ in. thick; cut eyes ⅜ in. wide, roll small ball pupils and nose. Roll thin logs for teeth (cut jagged edge with knife) and eyebrows. Melt light cocoa candy and add some white candy to lighten. Mix in coconut (use 7 oz. coconut per 14 oz. candy). Dip pop to cover; use fingers to shape pointed ears. Attach features while still wet. Chill in stand until firm.

b pop-eyed pops

PAN
9 x 13 x 2 in. Sheet

TIP
1

COLORS*
Golden Yellow, Lemon Yellow

FONDANT
White Ready-To-Use Rolled Fondant (⅛ oz. per treat),
9 in. Rolling Pin, Roll & Cut Mat, Brush Set, Oval Cut-Outs

CANDY*
White, Spooky Green, Midnight Black, Lavender, Orange Candy Melts, Chocolate Pro Melting Pot, Primary (yellow, orange) Candy Color Sets

RECIPE
Favorite Cake Ball Pops, p. 7

ALSO
6 in. Cookie Treat Sticks, Parchment Triangles, Pops Decorating Stand, black shoestring licorice, scissors, knife, ruler, tape

INSTRUCTIONS
Prepare medium cake balls and insert sticks following recipe. Chill. Dip in melted candy. Place in Decorating Stand; chill until firm. For eyes, tint small amount of fondant yellow. Roll out white and yellow fondant 1/16 in. thick. Cut eyes using smallest oval Cut-Out; attach to pop using melted candy. Fill parchment bag with melted black candy; tape tip 1 to outside of bag. Pipe dot mouth and eyes. Cut ¾ in. licorice pieces for hair. Attach 7-8 to each head with melted candy, holding in position until set.

*Combine Golden Yellow with Lemon Yellow for yellow fondant shown. Add orange candy color to melted orange candy and yellow candy color to melted yellow candy for darker shades shown.

Wilto

c) carved cut-ups

PAN
x 13 x 2 in. Sheet
P

CANDY*
White, Midnight Black, Orange
andy Melts; Primary (orange)
andy Color Set, Candy Eyeballs,
hocolate Pro Melting Pot

RECIPE
avorite Cake Ball Pops, p. 7

LSO
in. Cookie Treat Sticks, Pops
ecorating Stand, Parchment
iangles, small green spice
rops, tape

INSTRUCTIONS
Prepare medium cake balls and insert sticks following recipe; chill until firm. Dip cake balls in melted candy. Place in Decorating Stand; chill until firm. Tape tip 1 to outside of parchment bag; pipe noses, mouths, cheeks and eye sockets with melted candy; chill until firm. Attach Candy Eyeballs and spice drop half for stem using melted candy; chill.

*Add orange candy color to melted orange candy for darker orange shown.

d) boo to you too

PAN
x 13 x 2 in. Sheet

CANDY*
White, Midnight Black, Yellow
andy Melts, Candy Eyeballs,
hocolate Pro Melting Pot

RECIPES
avorite Cake Ball Pops, p. 7

LSO
ps Decorating Stand, 6 in.
ookie Treat Sticks, Parchment
iangles, black shoestring
orice, bumpy chenille pipe
eaners (12 in. lengths), knife,
ler

INSTRUCTIONS
Prepare large cake balls and insert sticks following recipe. Chill. Dip in melted candy. Place in Decorating Stand; chill until firm. Using melted black candy in cut parchment bag, attach eyes, pipe mouth and eyebrows. Cut 9 pieces of licorice, 1½ to 2 in. long; attach for hair using melted candy. Use melted yellow candy in cut parchment bag to pipe teeth. Wrap pipe cleaner around stick and shape hands.

ⓐ hand-held haunters

PAN
Silicone Round Brownie Pops Mold, Cookie Sheet

CANDY
White, Midnight Black Candy Melts, Candy Eyeballs, Chocolate Pro Melting Pot

ALSO
Pops Decorating Stand, 6 in. Cookie Treat Sticks, Parchment Triangles

INSTRUCTIONS
Bake and cool brownies in silicone mold supported by cookie sheet. Insert sticks following pops recipe (p. 7). Chill. Dip in melted candy. Place in Decorating Stand; chill until firm. Attach eyes. Use black candy in cut parchment bag to pipe mouth.

ⓑ fanged flyers

PANS
9 x 13 x 2 in. Sheet, Non-Stick Cookie Sheet, Cooling Grid

CANDY
White, Dark Cocoa, Midnight Black, Orange Candy Melts, Chocolate Pro Melting Pot

RECIPE
Favorite Cake Ball Pops, p. 7

ALSO
Heart Nesting Cookie Cutter Set, 8 in. Cookie Treat Sticks, Parchment Triangles, Parchment Paper; Pops Decorating Stand, chocolate chips, tape, scissors

INSTRUCTIONS
In advance: Make 2 wings for each treat. Line pan with parchment paper and position 2nd smallest heart cutter; fill ⅛ in. deep with melted cocoa candy. Chill until firm.

Prepare medium cake balls. Insert sticks following recipe; chill. Dip pops in melted cocoa candy. Place in Decorating Stand; chill until firm. Cut wings with knife to conform to curve of pop. Attach with melted candy; chill until firm. Attach chocolate chip ears; chill. Using melted candy in cut parchment bag, pipe dot eyes, pupils and nose, outline smile, wings and pull-out fangs. Chill until firm.

ⓒ seeing red

PAN
9 x 13 x 2 in. Sheet

TIPS
1, 2A, 190

COLORS*
Leaf Green, Lemon Yellow, Orange, Violet, Rose, Black

FONDANT
White Ready-To-Use Rolled Fondant (¼ oz. per treat), 9 in. Rolling Pin, Roll & Cut Mat, Brush Set

RECIPE
Favorite Cake Ball Pops, p. 7

ALSO
White Candy Dips, Red Candy Melts, Chocolate Pro Melting Pot, Pops Decorating Stand, 6 in. Cookie Treat Sticks, Parchment Triangles, knife, ruler, tape

INSTRUCTIONS
Prepare medium cake balls and insert sticks following recipe. Chill. Dip in melted candy. Place in Decorating Stand; chill until firm. Tint fondant and roll out ⅛ in. thick. Use wide end of tip 190 to cut colored eyes; use narrow end of tip 2A to cut black pupils. Attach using melted candy. Tape tip 1 to outside of parchment bag. Use melted red candy to pipe blood vessels; chill until set.

*Combine Violet with Rose for violet shown.

Eerie and eye-catching! Bloodshot eye pops are just the type of gross-out goodies kids crave on Halloween. With their bright fondant pupils and red candy capillaries, they're a great choice for bringing new colors to your terrifying treat table.

d ⃝ frank 'n pops

PAN
9 x 13 x 2 in. Sheet

CANDY
Spooky Green, Midnight Black Candy Melts, Chocolate Pro Melting Pot, Candy Eyeballs

ALSO
Pops Decorating Stand, 6 in. Cookie Treat Sticks, knife, ruler, mini candy-coated chocolates

INSTRUCTIONS
Prepare cereal treats and press firmly into prepared pan 1 in. deep. Cut 1¼ x 1¾ in. high heads. Dip sticks in melted candy, insert in heads. Chill. Dip in melted tinted candy. Place in Decorating Stand; chill until firm. Add drop of water to ¼ cup melted green candy. Working quickly, use cut parchment bag to pipe noses; attach eyes then pipe eyebrows or bags under eyes. Use melted black candy to pipe hair, mouth and forehead scar. Attach mini candy bolts.

a) fright by candlelight!

...N
...x 13 x 2 in. Sheet

...ANDY
...hite Candy Melts, Silver Foil
...rappers, Chocolate Pro Melting
...ot

...CIPE
...vorite Cake Ball Pops,
...hocolate recommended) p. 7

...SO
...hite Plastic Dowel Rods,
...rchment Triangles, 8 in. Cookie
...eat Sticks, Pops Treat Sticks
...pks.), Neon Colors Fondant
...ulti Pack, 13 ct. Cupcakes-N-
...re Stand, black shoestring
...orice, craft foam blocks,
...ue stick

INSTRUCTIONS
In advance: Make candles. Cut
dowel rods in eleven 4 in. lengths.
Pack cake ball mixture firmly into
dowel rods. Insert cookie sticks all
the way through. Chill until firm
then push out using stick. Dip in
melted candy; tap to settle. Insert in
craft blocks; chill until firm.

Wrap Pop Treat Sticks handles with
silver wrappers; secure with glue stick.
Remove cookie sticks from candles by
twisting out. Using melted candy in
cut parchment bag, fill opening in
candles and position on Pops Treat
Sticks; chill. Pipe dripping wax on top
and sides of candles and base of treat
sticks with melted candy; chill. For
flames, roll together small portions
of yellow and orange fondant to
marbleize. Roll ⅜ in. balls and taper
to form flame shape. Insert 1 in.
lengths of licorice for wicks into
flames, insert in candles. Position
candles in stand, sliding treat stick
handles through spirals and securing
with melted candy.

b)

b) wicked looks

...N
...x 13 x 2 in. Sheet

...LORS*
...ack, Violet, Rose, Orange, Leaf
...een, Lemon Yellow

...NDANT
...hite Ready-To-Use Rolled
...ondant (2½ oz. per treat), 9 in.
...lling Pin, Roll & Cut Mat, Brush
...t, Gum-Tex

...ANDY
...hite Candy Melts, Primary
...llow), Garden (green, black)
...ndy Color Sets, Chocolate Pro
...lting Pot

...CIPE
...vorite Cake Ball Pops, p. 7

...SO
...n. Cookie Treat Sticks, 101
...okie Cutters Set (smallest
...nd cutter used), Parchment
...angles, Pops Decorating Stand,
...fe, cornstarch

INSTRUCTIONS
In advance: Make hat. Roll out black
fondant ⅛ in. thick; cut brim using
smallest round cutter. Roll a 1⅛ in.
black ball into a 2 in. high cone;
attach to brim with damp brush. Let
set. For hat band, roll out violet
fondant 1/16 in. thick; cut a 2 x ¼ in.
wide long strip. Attach around hat
with damp brush. Use melted candy
in cut parchment bag to pipe buckle.

Prepare medium cake balls and
insert sticks following recipe; chill
until firm. Dip cake balls in melted
candy. Place in Decorating Stand;
chill until firm. Use melted candy in
cut parchment bag to pipe mouth,
eyes, pupils, eyebrows and tooth.
Shape a ½ in. long green fondant
nose and two ⅛ in. diameter fondant balls for warts. Attach with
melted candy; chill. Make hair. Tint
½ oz. fondant orange; knead in ⅛
teaspoon Gum-Tex. Roll out ⅛ in.
thick; cut 1½ x ⅛ in. wide strips. Let
dry on cornstarch-dusted surface for
5-10 minutes. Attach hair and hat
with melted candy; chill.

*Combine Violet with Rose for violet shown. Combine Leaf
  Green with Lemon Yellow for green shown.

c)

c) wrapped attention

...NS
...cone Boy Mold, 9 x 13 x 2 in.
...eet, Cookie Sheet, Cooling
...d

...NDY
...ite Candy Melts, Candy
...balls

...CIPE
...vorite Cake Ball Pops, p. 7

...SO
...ps Decorating Stand, 6 in.
...okie Treat Sticks, Parchment
...angles, knife, ruler

INSTRUCTIONS
Prepare cake ball mixture and
press into silicone mold. Chill then
unmold following recipe. Ice backs
with melted candy; let set. Place
candy side down on cooling grid
over cookie sheet. Pour on melted
candy to cover. Chill. Using melted
candy in cut parchment bag, drizzle
candy back and forth over mummies
for bandages. Change directions for
wrapped effect. Attach eyes with
melted candy. Use knife tip to
cut opening at bottom. Insert stick,
securing with candy.

autumn apples

PAN
9 x 13 x 2 in. Sheet

CANDY
Peanut Butter Candy Melts, Chocolate Pro Melting Pot

RECIPES
Favorite Cake Ball Pops, p. 7

ALSO
Parchment Paper, 6 in. Cookie Treat Sticks, chopped nuts, knife, ruler

INSTRUCTIONS
Prepare large cake balls and insert sticks following recipe. Chill. Dip in melted candy. Immediately roll in chopped nuts to cover bottom ½ to ¾ of pop. Set on parchment paper and chill until firm.

b gobble 'em up!

PAN
9 x 13 x 2 in. Sheet

COLORS*
Christmas Red, Red-Red, Lemon Yellow, Golden Yellow, Orange, Brown

FONDANT
White Ready-To-Use Rolled Fondant, 9 in. Rolling Pin, Roll & Cut Mat, Brush Set, Oval Cut-Outs

CANDY
Light Cocoa Candy Melts, Garden (black) Candy Color Set, Chocolate Pro Melting Pot

RECIPE
Favorite Cake Ball Pops, p. 7

ALSO
Pops Decorating Stand, 6 in. Cookie Treat Sticks, Parchment Triangles, Gum-Tex, knife, ruler

INSTRUCTIONS
In advance: Make tail feathers. Add ½ teaspoon Gum-Tex to 4 oz. fondant. Divide into 4 portions and tint red, yellow, brown and orange. Roll out ⅛ in. thick. Cut ovals using medium Cut-Out. Move Cut-Out to cut 1¼ x ½ in. feathers. Reserve brown and excess fondant. Let dry 24 hours.

Prepare large cake balls and insert sticks following recipe. Chill. Dip in melted candy. Place in Decorating Stand; chill until firm. Roll out brown fondant ⅛ in. thick. Cut 1¼ x ¾ in. wide wings and shape 1½ in. high neck and head; trim to shape using knife. Attach using melted candy. Shape beak and waddle from reserved fondant; attach. Pipe black dot eyes using tinted candy in cut parchment bag. Attach tail feathers with light cocoa candy.

*Combine Christmas Red with Red-Red for red shown. Combine Lemon Yellow with Golden Yellow for yellow shown. Combine Brown with Red-Red for Brown fondant shown.

c giving thanks together

PAN
9 x 13 x 2 in. Sheet

COLORS*
Lemon Yellow, Golden Yellow, Christmas Red, Black

FONDANT
White Ready-To-Use Rolled Fondant (1 oz. per treat), 9 in. Rolling Pin, Roll & Cut Mat, Brush Set, Leaf, Round Cut-Outs, Primary Fine Tip FoodWriter Edible Color Markers

CANDY*
White, Light Cocoa Candy Melts; Primary (yellow, orange, red), Garden (black) Candy Color Sets, Chocolate Pro Melting Pot

RECIPE
Favorite Cake Ball Pops, p. 7

ALSO
Pops Decorating Stand, 6 in. Cookie Treat Sticks, Parchment Triangles; knife, ruler, scissors

INSTRUCTIONS
In advance: Make feathers. Tint fondant yellow. Roll out 1/16 in. thick. Cut using smallest leaf Cut-Out. Let dry. Draw veins using red FoodWriter.

Prepare medium cake balls and insert sticks following recipe. Chill. Dip in melted, tinted candy. Place in Decorating Stand; chill until firm. Use melted candy in cut parchment bags to pipe hair on both Pilgrims. Tint fondant assorted colors and roll out 1/16 in. thick as needed. Decorate pops as described below. Attach trims using damp brush. Use melted candy in cut parchment bags to pipe dot nose and eyes, outline brows and smiles.

Male Native American: For hair, cut a 2½ x 3 in. long black fondant heart. Attach. Use knife to indent across top for hair. Use scissors to cut back bottom straight; cut thin vertical slits for strands of hair. Cut a 3/16 x 4 in. yellow fondant strip; attach around head. Attach feather using small fondant ball. **Female Native American:** For hair, cut a 2½ x 2 in. long black fondant heart. Attach. Use knife to indent across top for hair. Use knife to cut back bottom short. For braids, roll 3 thin logs, 1½ in. long. Twist together and attach. Cut red fondant strips ⅛ in. wide for bands; attach. Cut a 3/16 x 4 in. yellow fondant strip; attach around head. Attach feather using small fondant ball. **Male Pilgrim:** For black fondant hat, cut brim using medium round Cut-Out. Shape ⅝ x ⅞ in. diameter top; attach to brim. Cut ⅛ x 2½ in. gray fondant strip; attach for hat band. Use knife to cut 5/16 x ¼ in. high yellow fondant buckle; attach. Attach hat using melted candy in cut parchment bag. **Female Pilgrim:** Roll a 1 in. ball of fondant; flatten and attach to back of head. Using white fondant, cut a 3 x 3½ in. wide strip for hat. Fold ½ in. over for front brim and attach. For bow, cut 2 streamers, ¼ x 1¼ in. long; attach to stick. Cut 2 strips for loops, ¼ x 2 in. Cut a ¼ x ½ in. strip for knot; wrap around loops and attach to streamers.

*Combine Lemon Yellow with Golden Yellow for yellow fondant shown. Use orange candy color for pilgrims' skin tone. Combine white and light cocoa candy for Native Americans' skin tone.

Wilt

d) corn cop

AN
x 13 x 2 in. Sheet

OLORS*
elly Green, Red-Red, Brown

ONDANT
White Ready-To-Use Rolled Fondant, 9 in. Rolling Pin, Roll &
ut Mat, Brush Set, 10 Pc. Fondant/Gum Paste Tool Set

ANDY*
eanut Butter, White Candy Melts, Primary (yellow), Garden
lack) Candy Color Sets, Foil Candy Cups, Chocolate Pro
elting Pot, Candy Eyeballs

ECIPE
avorite Cake Ball Pops, p. 7

LSO
ops Decorating Stand, 6 in. Cookie Treat Sticks, Cake Boards,
archment Triangles, Parchment Paper, knife, ruler

STRUCTIONS
advance: Prepare candy trims. For collar, flatten foil cup and
rush on melted peanut butter candy; chill until firm. Melt some
hite candy and tint yellow. Use cut parchment bag to pipe
–30 straw hairs ¾ to 1 in. long on parchment-covered board.
ake extras to allow for breakage and let set.

epare large cake balls and insert sticks following recipe. Chill
ntil firm. Dip in melted candy. Place in Decorating Stand until
t. Use heated knife tip to cut hole in center of collar. Remove
il and slide onto stick; secure with melted candy. Roll out red
ndant ¹⁄₁₆ in. thick. Cut a ³⁄₈ in. triangle for nose. Use tinted black
ndy in cut parchment bag to pipe mouth. Attach nose, eyes
d hair with melted candy. For hat, shape a 1½ in. green ball
to a mound. Use cone tool from set to shape a 1 ¼ in. high
own. Roll edge thin with modeling stick to shape a 2½ in.
ameter brim. Attach to pop with melted candy. Roll out brown
ndant ¹⁄₁₆ in. thick. Cut a ¼ in. wide strip for hat band; attach
ing damp brush.

ombine Kelly Green with a little Brown for green fondant shown. Combine Brown with Red-Red for brown
ndant shown. Combine equal portions of White and Peanut Butter Candy Melts for face color shown.

d

e) autumn leaves

PANS
10.5 x 15.5 x 1 in. Jelly Roll

COLOR
Brown

CANDY
Green, Orange, Red, Yellow, Light Cocoa Candy Melts,
Chocolate Pro Melting Pot

RECIPE
Pound Cake from a Cake Mix, p. 7

ALSO
9 Pc. Leaves and Acorns Nesting Cutter Set; Parchment
Triangles; Pops Decorating Stand, 6 in. Cookie Treat Sticks;
knife, ruler, shredded coconut, 3½ in. woven basket, 2 x 2 x
3 in. craft foam block, zip-close plastic bag

INSTRUCTIONS
Bake and cool cake; level to 1 in. high. Cut assorted leaves using
smallest cutters from set. Dip cookie stick in melted candy and insert.
Chill. Dip in melted candy. Place in Decorating Stand; chill until firm.
Use contrasting colors of melted candy in cut parchment bags to pipe
veins. Chill until firm. Tint coconut. Place a small amount of coconut in
plastic bag. Add a little brown icing color. Close bag and knead to tint.
Insert craft block in basket; cover with coconut. Insert pops.

ww.wilton.com

(a) tree flocking

PANS
9 x 13 x 2 in. Sheet, Silicone Boy Mold, Cookie Sheet, Cooling Grid

CANDY
Green, Light Cocoa, White Candy Melts

RECIPES
Roll-Out Cookies, Favorite Cake Ball Pops, p. 7

ALSO
3 Pc. Trees Metal Cutter Set, White Sparkling Sugar, Pops Display Stand, 6 in. Cookie Treat Sticks, Disposable Decorating Bags, Parchment Triangles, Parchment Paper, knife, ruler, white construction paper, shredded coconut, spice drops, mint discs, scissors, glue stick

INSTRUCTIONS
For trees, prepare and roll out cookie dough. Cut using classic fir tree from set. Bake and cool cookies. Attach sticks to backs using melted candy. For people, prepare cake ball mixture. Press into mold, chill then unmold. Insert sticks following recipe. Chill. Ice back side with melted candy; chill until firm. Place tree cookies on cooling grid over parchment-covered cookie sheet. Cover with melted candy using cut disposable bag (add white to green and light cocoa candy for lighter shades shown; tap to settle then chill until set. For people, pipe details and fill in areas using melted candy in cut parchment bag. Pipe zigzag bands on trees; immediately sprinkle on sugar. Position in stand. Cut snow from paper; attach to stand with glue stick. Sprinkle coconut on stand. Attach spice drops with melted candy.

(b) pinwheel pops

PANS
Round Pops Cookie Pan, Cookie Sheet, Cooling Grid

RECIPES
Vanilla Sugar Cookies on a Stick, p. 7

ALSO
Red, Green, White Candy Melts, Pops Decorating Stand, 6 in. Cookie Treat Sticks, Parchment Triangles, knife, ruler

INSTRUCTIONS
Prepare dough. Bake and cool cookies in pan with sticks. Place on cooling grid over cookie sheet. Cover with melted white candy. Let set. Use melted candy in cut parchment bags to pipe pinwheel pattern.

With spice drop earmuffs and an ear-resistible smile, these snowmen friends are sure to melt their hearts! It's an easy-to-decorate design that makes a perfect stocking stuffer.

c ear-resistible snowmen

PAN
9 x 13 x 2 in. Sheet

CANDY
White Candy Dips, Garden (black) Candy Color Set

RECIPES
Favorite Cake Ball Pops, p. 7

ALSO
Parchment Triangles, 6 in. Cookie Treat Sticks, Pops Decorating Stand, black shoestring licorice, spice drops, knife, ruler

INSTRUCTIONS
Prepare small cake balls and insert sticks following recipe. Chill. Dip in melted candy. Place in Decorating Stand; chill until firm. Using candy color, tint a small amount of melted white candy black. Pipe dot eyes and outline mouth using melted candy in cut parchment bag. Cut and shape cone for nose using a piece of spice drop; attach with melted candy. For ear muffs, cut spice drop halves; insert 2 in. licorice strings. Attach with melted candy.

d toy-making team

PAN
9 x 13 x 2 in. Sheet

TIPS
3, 5

COLOR
Orange

FONDANT
Primary Colors (green, red) Fondant Multi Pack, 9 in. Rolling Pin, Roll & Cut Mat, Brush Set, Daisy Cut-Outs, Gum-Tex

CANDY
White Candy Melts, Garden (black), Primary (orange) Candy Color Sets, Chocolate Pro Melting Pot

RECIPES
Favorite Cake Ball Pops, Royal Icing, p. 7

ALSO
Pops Decorating Stand, 6 in. Cookie Treat Sticks, Meringue Powder, knife, ruler

INSTRUCTIONS
In advance: Make collars. Add ⅛ teaspoon Gum-Tex to 2 oz. red fondant. Roll out ¹⁄₁₆ in. thick. Cut using medium daisy Cut-Out. Make hole in center using cookie stick. Let dry overnight.

Prepare medium cake balls and insert sticks following recipe. Chill. Dip in melted candy. Place in Decorating Stand; chill until firm. For hats, roll a 1¼ in. diameter red ball for Santa, a 1⅛ in. diameter green ball for elves. Shape into cones, 2½ in. high for Santa, 2 in. high for elves. Attach using melted candy in cut parchment bag. Use melted candy to pipe outline smiles and dot eyes. Use icing to pipe tip 5 zigzag hat trims and beard, tip 3 bead mustache and outline eyebrows. Tint a small portion of icing to match skin tone shown. Pipe tip 5 pull-out dot ears and tip 3 dot noses. Slide on collars and secure with icing.

e downhill duo

PANS
9 x 13 x 2 in. Sheet, Silicone Boy Mold; Cookie Sheet, Cooling Grid

COLORS*
Leaf Green, Christmas Red, Red-Red, Royal Blue, Black

FONDANT
White Ready-To-Use Rolled Fondant (1 oz. per treat); 9 in. Rolling Pin; Roll & Cut Mat; Gum-Tex

CANDY*
Red, Blue, White, Light Cocoa Candy Melts; Garden (green, black), Primary (yellow) Candy Color Sets

RECIPE
Favorite Cake Ball Pops, p. 7

ALSO
6 in. Cookie Treat Sticks; Parchment Triangles, Parchment Paper, Cake Boards; black shoestring licorice, knife, cornstarch

INSTRUCTIONS
In advance: Make fondant trims. Knead in ¼ teaspoon Gum-Tex per 4 oz. fondant for four treats. Tint 1 oz. blue, green and red, ½ oz. black. Roll out ⅛ in. thick. Cut ¼ x 2½ in. skis; trim a point on one end. Shape a curl at pointed end and let dry on cornstarch-dusted board, supporting with Cookie Treat Stick. For hats, roll a ¾ in. ball of fondant; shape into a cone and point end to side. Let dry on cornstarch-dusted board.

Prepare cake pops recipe; press into mold cavities and chill until firm. Insert sticks following recipe; chill. Ice back of treat with melted candy; chill until firm. Set treat candy side down on cooling grid over parchment-covered cookie sheet. Pour on melted candy in desired skin tone; tap to settle and chill until firm. Using melted candy in cut parchment bag, pipe in snowsuit; chill until firm. Roll out black fondant ⅛ in. thick; cut 1 x 1½ in. strips for boots. Roll ⅜ in. ball for gloves. Using melted candy in cut parchment bag, attach gloves, hat; pipe swirl and pull-out hair, dot and string facial features, buttons, cuffs, hat brim and pull-out pompom. Chill until firm. Roll out fondant ⅛ in. thick. Cut a ³⁄₁₆ x 4½ in. long strip for scarf. Cut slits for fringe and attach around skier with melted candy. For ski poles, cut 1¾ in. licorice pieces. Roll and flatten ¼ in. circles for ski pole baskets; insert on licorice, securing with melted candy. Attach skis and poles with melted candy.

*Combine Christmas Red with Red-Red for red shown. Combine orange or light cocoa candy with melted white candy for skin tones shown.

a) sugar canes

PANS
9 x 13 x 2 in. Sheet, Cookie Sheet, Cooling Grid

CANDY
Red, White Candy Melts

RECIPE
Favorite Cake Ball Pops, p. 7

ALSO
Red Colored Sugar, Plastic Dowel Rods (cut to 4 in. lengths), 6 in. Cookie Treat Sticks, Parchment Triangles, Disposable Decorating Bags, Cake Boards, 9 in. Angled Spatula, Parchment Paper, knife, ruler

INSTRUCTIONS
Prepare cake ball mixture. Pack firmly into plastic dowel rods. Insert cookie treat stick 2½ in. into dowel rod. Chill completely, then push up stick to release. Gently shape top curve of cane. Chill. Ice back with melted candy; set on parchment-covered board and chill until set. Place canes on cooling grid over parchment-covered cookie sheet. Cover with melted candy using cut disposable bag. Tap to settle then chill until set. Use melted red candy in cut parchment bag to pipe ½ in. wide stripes; immediately sprinkle on red sugar. Chill until firm.

b) voices like angels

PAN
9 x 13 x 2 in. Sheet

TIPS
1, 3

COLORS*
Lemon Yellow, Black, Brown, Red-Red

CANDY
White, Light Cocoa Candy Melts, Primary (orange, red) Candy Color Set, Chocolate Pro Melting Pot

RECIPES
Favorite Cake Ball Pops, Royal Icing, p. 7

ALSO
Pops Decorating Stand, Gold Pearl Dust, Brush Set, Imitation Clear Vanilla Extract, 6 in. Cookie Treat Sticks, Meringue Powder, Parchment Triangles; knife, ruler, tape

INSTRUCTIONS
Reserve 1 white Candy Melt for each pop. Prepare medium cake balls and insert sticks following recipe. Chill. Dip in melted candy. Place in Decorating Stand; chill until firm. Decorate using royal icing. Pipe tip 3 swirl-motion curly hair. Use tip 1 to pipe outline eyes; outline and fill in mouth (pat smooth with finger). For halo, paint edge of reserved white candy disk with Pearl Dust/vanilla mixture; let dry. Attach using icing.

*Combine Brown with Red-Red for brown hair shown. For light skin tone, use white candy with a little orange candy color. For dark skin tone, use light cocoa and white candy with a little red candy color.

Wilto

c winter's first flakes

PAN
9 x 13 x 2 in. Sheet

RECIPE
Favorite Cake Ball Pops, p. 7

CANDY
Light Cocoa, White Candy Melts, Chocolate Pro Melting Pot

ALSO
Parchment Triangles, Pops Decorating Stand, 6 in. Cookie Treat Sticks

INSTRUCTIONS
Prepare large cake pops. Insert stick following recipe; chill until firm. Dip pops into melted candy. Place in Decorating Stand; chill until firm. Use cut parchment bag and melted white Candy Melts to pipe snowflake design on pop. Let set. Each serves 1.

d frozen folks

PAN
9 x 13 x 2 in. Sheet

TIP
2

COLORS*
Kelly Green, Violet, Rose, Red-Red, Christmas Red, Orange, Black

FONDANT
White Ready-To-Use Rolled Fondant (1 oz. per treat); 9 in. Rolling Pin; Roll & Cut Mat

CANDY
White Candy Melts, Chocolate Pro Melting Pot

RECIPES
Favorite Cake Ball Pops, Buttercream Icing, p. 7

ALSO
8 in. Lollipop Sticks, ruler, knife, toothpick, craft foam block

INSTRUCTIONS
Prepare cake balls using medium for body and 1 in. diameter for head. Insert stick in medium ball and toothpick in 1 in. ball following recipe, chill until firm. Dip cake balls in melted candy; tap to settle. Insert in craft foam block; chill until firm. Remove head from toothpick and attach to body with melted candy; chill.

For scarves, roll out fondant ⅛ in. thick. Cut 6 x ¼ in. strips. Wrap around neck; trim as needed and secure with melted candy. Make cone fondant hats, 1½ in. diameter at base, tapering to approximately ¼ in. at top and 1½ in. tall. Shape as desired; attach to head with melted candy. Using buttercream and tip 2, pipe dot eyes, noses, buttons and outline mouth. Pipe tip 2 swirl-motion brim and pompom.

*Combine Violet with Rose for violet shown. Combine Christmas Red with Red-Red for red shown.

e tree traditions

PAN
9 x 13 x 2 in. Sheet

TIPS
2, 4, 6, 8, 10, 12

COLORS*
Christmas Red, Red-Red, Violet, Rose, Lemon Yellow, Kelly Green, Royal Blue

FONDANT
White Ready-To-Use Rolled Fondant, 9 in. Rolling Pin, Roll & Cut Mat, Brush Set, Silver, White Pearl Dust

CANDY
White Candy Dips, Red, Green Candy Melts

RECIPES
Favorite Cake Ball Pops, Royal Icing, p. 7

ALSO
Silver Pearl Dust, White Sugar Pearls, Pops Decorating Stand, 6 in. Lollipop Sticks, Meringue Powder, Parchment Triangles, Imitation Clear Vanilla Extract, knife, ruler

INSTRUCTIONS
Prepare small cake balls and insert sticks following recipe. Chill. Dip in melted white Candy Dips. Place in Decorating Stand; chill until firm. Tint fondant assorted colors and roll out 1/16 in. thick as needed. Decorate balls as described below. Use damp brush to attach fondant; use icing to attach Sugar Pearls. For hanger, roll a ½ in. ball of fondant; flatten into ¼ thick disk. Slide onto stick. Use icing to secure disk and pipe tip 2 curved top hook. Paint hanger and hook with silver Pearl Dust/vanilla mixture. Paint white areas with white Pearl Dust.

Blue and violet stripes: Cut 5 blue and 5 violet fondant strips, ¼ x 1¾ in long. Attach with slight curve. Trim ends as needed. **Yellow:** Cut a ⅜ x 5 in. yellow fondant strip and attach around center. Attach pearls. **Green tree:** Cut a 1¼ in. high green fondant tree; attach to front. Cut a ⅛ x 4 in. red fondant strip. Shape and attach for bow. Roll small ball for knot; attach. Pipe tip 2 icing dot ornaments. **Green with red scrolls:** Cut a ¼ x 5 in. green fondant strip; attach around center. Cut ⅛ x 5 in. strips of red and yellow fondant; attach above and below green. Trim using melted candy in cut parchment bags: Pipe 6 red scrolls on green and green dots on red. Attach pearls between scrolls. **Blue dots:** Cut blue fondant dots using narrow end of tips 4, 6, 8, 10 and 12; attach in 6 rows of decreasing size.

*Combine Christmas Red with Red-Red for red shown. Combine Violet with Rose for violet shown.

pop culture

Even at the fanciest receptions, everyone goes for the finger food. Pops fit right in! Decorated pops make the ideal sweet table treat—they're convenient to eat, can be styled to complement your colors and theme and they stand up to create a display every guest will be talking about. A reception pop design can range from a simple dip in sparkling sugar or marbleized candy to an adorable shower teddy bear or a tiered wedding cake. As you're about to see, pops have the power to make a big impression at your next big event!

Wilto

a baby block pops

PANS
10.5 x 15.5 x 1 in. Jelly Roll, Cooling Grid

COLORS*
Rose, Sky Blue, Kelly Green, Lemon Yellow, Golden Yellow

FONDANT
White Ready-To-Use Rolled Fondant (½ oz. per treat), 9 in. Rolling Pin, Roll & Cut Mat, Brush Set, Alphabet/Number Cut-Outs

CANDY
White Candy Melts, Garden (pink, green), Primary (yellow, blue) Candy Color Sets, Chocolate Pro Melting Pot

RECIPE
Pound Cake from a Cake Mix, p.7

ALSO
Pops Decorating Stand, 6 in. Lollipop Sticks, Parchment Triangles; knife, ruler

INSTRUCTIONS
Bake and cool cake; trim to 1 in. high. Cut into 1 in. squares. Insert sticks following cake pops recipe (p. 7). Chill. Dip in melted candy. Place in Decorating Stand; chill until firm. Pipe borders using melted, tinted candy in cut parchment bags. Let set. Tint fondant and roll out 1/16 in. thick. Cut letters. Attach using damp brush.

*Combine Lemon Yellow with Golden Yellow for yellow fondant shown.

b cuddly cubs

PAN
3-D Mini Bear

TIPS
2A, 12

COLORS
Sky Blue, Rose

FONDANT
White Ready-To-Use Rolled Fondant (½ oz. per treat), 9 in. Rolling Pin, Roll & Cut Mat

CANDY
White Candy Melts, Primary (yellow, blue) and Garden (pink, black) Candy Color Sets, Chocolate Pro Melting Pot

ALSO
8 in. Lollipop Sticks, Parchment Triangles, Pops Decorating Stand; knife

INSTRUCTIONS
Bake and cool bears following package directions. Insert sticks following pops recipe directions (p. 7); chill. Dip in melted candy; tap to settle. Place pops in Decorating Stand; chill until firm. Roll out fondant 1/8 in. thick. Cut the following in white, blue or rose fondant: For inner ears, cut circles with narrow end of tip 12; cut in half. For muzzles and paw pads, cut circles using narrow end of tip 2A. For bibs, cut circles with wide end of tip 12; move up tip and cut a scallop to conform to neck. Attach all with melted candy. Using melted tinted candy in cut parchment bag, pipe facial features, duck and dot bib border; chill until firm.

c rockin' babies

PAN
9 x 13 x 2 in. Sheet

FONDANT
White Ready-To-Use Rolled Fondant (½ oz. per treat), 9 in. Rolling Pin, Roll & Cut Mat, Brush Set, Round Cut-Outs

CANDY
White, Light Cocoa Candy Melts, Primary (orange, yellow), Garden (black) Candy Color Sets, Chocolate Pro Melting Pot

RECIPE
Favorite Cake Ball Pops, p. 7

ALSO
Blossom Plastic Nesting Cutter Set, Jumbo Confetti Sprinkles, Flowerful Medley Sprinkles (confetti), Pops Decorating Stand, 6 in. Cookie Treat Sticks, Parchment Triangles; 1/8 in. wide ribbon (10 in. for each pop), knife, ruler

INSTRUCTIONS
Prepare medium cake balls and insert sticks following recipe. Chill. Dip in melted, tinted candy. Place in Decorating Stand; chill until firm. Use melted candy in cut parchment bags to pipe hair curl and facial features (let mouth set before overpiping tooth). For bonnet base, roll out fondant 3/16 in. thick. Cut using medium round Cut-Out. Roll to make slightly larger. Attach to back of head using damp brush. For bonnet brim, roll out fondant 1/8 in. thick. Cut using 3rd largest blossom cutter. Cut in half. Use knife to trim bottom curve to conform to pop. Shorten center scallop and cut left and right scallops to look like 2 each. Attach using damp brush. With melted candy attach 1 jumbo and 1 regular size confetti to make pacifier. Tie ribbon around stick.

Wilt

(d) bow-tie bears

PAN
9 x 13 x 2 in. Sheet

TIPS
2A, 16

COLORS*
Kelly Green, Brown, Red-Red, Black

FONDANT
White Ready-To-Use Rolled Fondant
(½ oz. per treat), 9 in. Rolling Pin, Roll &
Cut Mat, Brush Set, Heart Cut-Outs

CANDY
Light Cocoa Candy Melts, Garden (black)
Candy Color Set, Chocolate Pro Melting Pot

RECIPE
Favorite Cake Ball Pops, p. 7

ALSO
Pops Decorating Stand, 8 in. Cookie Treat
Sticks, Parchment Triangles; knife, ruler

INSTRUCTIONS
Prepare medium cake balls and insert
sticks following recipe. Chill. Dip in
melted candy; tap to settle. Place in
Decorating Stand; chill until firm. Tint
fondant green, dark brown and tan; roll
out ⅛ in. thick as needed. Use wide end
of tip 16 to cut outer ear; trim bottom to
conform to head. Use narrow end of tip
2A to cut inner ear; trim and attach
using damp brush. Attach to pop with
melted candy. Use wide end of tip 16 to
cut muzzle; attach using damp brush.
For bow tie, cut 2 hearts using smallest
Cut-Out; attach using melted candy.
Roll small ball and flatten for knot;
attach using damp brush. Use tinted
black candy in cut parchment
bag to pipe eyes, nose and mouth.

*Combine Brown with Red-Red and Black for dark brown ears
shown.

(e) shower shakers

PAN
9 x 13 x 2 in. Sheet

FONDANT
White Ready-To-Use Rolled Fondant (½ oz.
per treat), 9 in. Rolling Pin, Brush Set

CANDY
White, Yellow Candy Melts, Garden (green)
Candy Color Set, Chocolate Pro Melting Pot

RECIPE
Favorite Cake Ball Pops, p. 7

ALSO
11¾ in. Lollipop Sticks, Jumbo Confetti
Sprinkles, Parchment Triangles, Pops
Decorating Stand; ¼ in. wide ribbon (10 in.
per pop), knife, ruler

INSTRUCTIONS
Prepare 1 large cake ball per treat;
insert sticks following recipe. Chill. Dip
in melted tinted candy. Place in
Decorating Stand; chill until firm. For
bottom of rattle, roll ⅞ in. diameter
fondant ball. Push a new stick in ball
and dip in melted candy; chill, then
twist stick and remove. Slide onto stick
2 in. below large pop; secure with dot
of melted candy. Use melted white
candy in cut parchment bag to pipe
½ in. wide band around large pop. Chill
until firm. Attach 10 confetti pieces to
band using dots of melted candy. Let
set. Tie on ribbon.

(f) cookie carriage

PANS
Round Pops Cookie Pan, Cookie Sheet,
Cooling Grid

TIP
3

RECIPES
Vanilla Sugar Cookies on a Stick, Color
Flow Icing, p. 7

ALSO
Color Flow Mix, White Sugar Pearls, 8 in.
Cookie Treat Sticks, Parchment Paper;
knife, ruler

INSTRUCTIONS
Prepare cookie dough and press into
pan. Bake and cool cookies with sticks.
Cut away slightly less than ¼ of cookie.
Set on cooling grid set over parchment-covered cookie sheet. Pour on
thinned icing; tap to settle then let dry
on parchment-covered surface. Use
full-strength icing to pipe tip 3 outlines
and to attach Sugar Pearls.

ⓐ wedding party

PAN
9 x 13 x 2 in. Sheet

COLORS
Rose, Black

FONDANT
White Ready-To-Use Rolled Fondant (½ oz. per treat), Flower Cut-Outs, 9 in. Rolling Pin, Roll & Cut Mat, Brush S Cutter/ Embosser, 10 Pc. Fondant/Gum Paste Tool Set, Fondant Shaping Foam

CANDY
White, Light Cocoa, Red, Yellow, Orange Candy Melts, Garden (black) Candy Color Set, Chocolate Pro Melting P

RECIPE
Favorite Cake Ball Pops, p. 7

ALSO
Pops Decorating Stand, White Sugar Pearls, 6 in. Cooki Treat Sticks, Parchment Triangles; knife, ruler, aluminur foil, toothpicks

INSTRUCTIONS
In advance: Make fondant trims. For veil, roll out fonda ⅛ in. thick. Cut a 2½ in. 3½ in. high triangle; trim ¾ in. o top point. Set on a crumpled foil ball, 1⅜ in. diameter; curl bottom ends and hold in place with more foil. Let dry. For flowers, roll out fondant 1/16 in. thick. Cut using smallest Cut-Out. Thin edges on thin foam and cup on thin foam using dogbone tool from set. For bow tie, ro two ½ in. fondant balls. Shape into triangles; use toothpick to add details. Roll small ball for center kno

Prepare medium cake balls and insert sticks following recipe. Chill. Dip in melted candy tinted to desired skin tones. Place in Decorating Stand; chill until firm. Use melted candy in cut parchment bags to pipe hair; add pull-out details using toothpick. Let set. Pipe dot eyes, pupils and noses. Pipe line lashes and groom's smile, bead heart lips for ladies. Attach fondant trims and Sugar Pearl flower centers using melted candy.

ⓑ a day for love

PANS
10.5 x 15.5 x 1 in. Jelly Roll, Cooling Grid

COLOR
Rose

FONDANT
White Ready-To-Use Rolled Fondant (¼ oz. per treat) Round Cut-Outs

CANDY
White Candy Melts, Hearts Candy Mold

RECIPE
Pound Cake from a Mix, p. 7

ALSO
Pops Doilies, Pops Decorating Stand, 6 in. Lollipop Sticks, Cake Boards, Parchment Triangles, Parchment Paper; knife, ruler, toothpicks, shortening

INSTRUCTIONS
In advance: Make fondant hearts. Use shortening to lightly grease candy mold cavities. Tint fondant. Press in cavities, unmold. Insert toothpick ½ in. into bottom of heart. Let dry flat on parchment-covered surface.

Bake and cool cake; trim to 1 in. high. Cut rounds using medium and large Cut-Outs. Set on cooling grid placed over parchment-covered pan. Pour on melted candy to cover. Tap to settle then move to parchment-covered board. Chill until set. Spread small amount of candy over doily; attach bottom cake. Attach top cake; chill until firm Cut small opening in bottom for stick and insert stick following cake pops recipe (p. 7). Place in Decorating Stand; chill until firm. Divide top cake into 6ths, bottom cake into 8ths. Add a drop of water to a small amount of melted candy to thicken. Working quickly, use cut parchment bag to pipe drop strings between marks. Pip bead borders and dot trims. Insert heart.

Wilt

ⓒ heart partners

PAN
9 x 13 x 2 in. Sheet, Silicone Petite Hearts Mold, Cookie Sheet, Cooling Grid

COLOR
Rose

FONDANT
White Ready-To-Use Rolled Fondant (½ oz. per treat), Natural Colors (pink, light brown, dark brown, black) Fondant Multi Pack, 9 in. Rolling Pin, Brush Set, Flower Cut-Outs, Fondant Shaping Foam, 10 Pc. Fondant/ Gum Paste Tool Set, White Pearl Dust, Brush Set

CANDY
White Candy Melts, Garden (pink), Primary (orange) Candy Color Sets, Chocolate Pro Melting Pot, White Jordan Almonds

RECIPES
Favorite Cake Ball Pops, Roll-Out Cookies, p. 7

ALSO
Hearts Metal Cutter Set, Metal Gingerbread Boy Cutter, Pops Display Stand, Pops Decorating Stand, 6 in. Cookie Treat Sticks, White Pearl Beading, Parchment Paper, Parchment Triangles; knife, ruler, silk flowers, glue stick

INSTRUCTIONS

In advance: Make cookies. Prepare and roll out dough. Cut large heart using largest cutter from set. Cut bride and groom using gingerbread boy cutter. Bake and cool cookies. Set cookies on cooling grid over parchment-lined cookie sheet. Pour on melted, tinted candy to cover. (We used orange candy color for skin tone shown.) Tap to settle; chill until firm. Attach sticks with melted candy. **Also:** Make fondant flowers. Tint fondant and roll out ¹⁄₁₆ in. thick. Cut 1 flower using medium Cut-Out; use small Cut-Out to cut 1 flower for each small heart. Cup centers on thick foam using small ball tool. Let dry.

For small hearts: Prepare cake pops mixture. Press into silicone mold; chill. Insert sticks following pops recipe. Chill. Dip in melted, tinted candy. Place in Decorating Stand; chill until firm. Use melted candy in cut parchment bag to attach flowers and to pipe dot center. **For large heart:** Use melted candy in cut parchment bag to attach flower, pipe dot center and attach stick to back. **For bride:** Roll out white fondant ¹⁄₁₆ in. thick. Cut 2½ x 1½ in. rectangle for skirt. Gather top long edge to form pleats. Lift bottom edge with modeling stick to shape. Cut bodice using cookie cutter as a guide. Cut 2 x ⅛ in. belt. Attach dress using melted candy. Brush belt and neckline with water; sprinkle with Pearl Dust. For hair, roll out fondant and cut ¼ in. wide strips, 1-2 in. long; attach. Cut a 1½ x 2¼ in. rectangle for veil; trim bottom to 2 in. wide. Attach veil. Roll 7 tiny balls and attach for tiara. Pipe nose with a dot of melted candy. Roll and attach facial features using damp brush. **For groom:** Roll out fondant ¹⁄₁₆ in. thick. Cut jacket, pants and shirt insert using cookie as a guide. Attach using melted candy. Cut tiny triangles for hair; attach. Cut bow tie; attach. Pipe nose with melted candy. Roll tiny buttons and facial features; attach using damp brush. Attach beading and silk flowers around edge of stand with glue stick. Insert pops in stand. Position Jordan Almonds.

with this ring...

PANS
10.5 x 15.5 x 1 in. Jelly Roll, Cooling Grid

CANDY
Yellow, White Candy Melts, Girl Power (ring) Candy Mold, Brush Set

RECIPE
Pound Cake from a Cake Mix, p. 7

ALSO
Round Cut-Outs, Pops Decorating Stand, 6 in. Lollipop Sticks, Cake Boards, Parchment Triangles, Parchment Paper, Imitation Clear Vanilla Extract, Gold Pearl Dust; knife, ruler

INSTRUCTIONS
In advance: Make candy diamonds. Use melted candy in cut parchment bag to mold just diamond and prongs in candy mold. Chill until set.

Bake and cool cake; trim to ¾ in. high. Cut rounds using medium Cut-Out. Ice bottoms with melted white candy. Chill until set then place candy-side down on cooling grid set over parchment-covered pan. Pour on melted white candy to cover top and sides. Chill until set. Use melted yellow candy in cut parchment bag to build up edge of ring and cover sides. Use knife tip to poke hole in bottom. Insert stick and secure with melted candy. Attach diamond. Place in Decorating Stand; chill until firm. Paint gold areas with Pearl Dust/vanilla mixture.

the golden touch

PANS
9 x 13 x 2 in. Sheet

CANDY
White, Light Cocoa Candy Melts, Chocolate Pro Melting Pot

RECIPES
Favorite Cake Ball Pops, p. 7

ALSO
Parchment Triangles, 6 in. Lollipop Sticks, Brush Set, Pops Decorating Stand, Gold Pearl Dust, Imitation Clear Vanilla Extract

INSTRUCTIONS
Prepare small cake balls and insert sticks following recipe. Chill. Dip in melted candy. Place in Decorating Stand; chill until firm. For white pops, brush with Pearl Dust/vanilla mixture; drizzle with melted light cocoa candy in cut parchment bag and let set. For cocoa pops, drizzle with melted white candy in cut parchment bag; let set. Brush drizzled area with Pearl Dust/vanilla mixture.

c grand monogram

PANS
Heart Pops Cookie Pan, Cookie Sheet, Cooling Grid

TIP
3

COLORS*
Violet, Rose, Black

FONDANT
White Ready-To-Use Rolled Fondant (2 oz. per treat), 9 in. Rolling Pin, Roll & Cut Mat, Brush Set

RECIPES
Vanilla Sugar Cookies on a Stick, Color Flow Icing, p. 7

ALSO
From the Heart Nesting Metal Cutter Set (large crinkle used), Blue Sugar Pearls, 9 in. Angled Spatula, 8 in. Cookie Treat Sticks, Color Flow Mix, Parchment Paper; knife, ruler

INSTRUCTIONS
Bake and cool cookies in cookie pan with sticks. Set on cooling grid over parchment-covered cookie sheet. Pour on violet tinted thinned icing to cover outer ridge; tap to settle. Use spatula to remove any excess icing from indentation. Let dry on parchment-covered surface. Roll out fondant ⅛ in. thick. Cut heart using large crinkle cutter from set. Brush back center with damp brush; position on cookie. Use fingers to lightly press from edge toward center to make edges curl up a bit; pinch crinkled edges with fingers to thin. Use full-strength icing to attach Sugar Pearls and pipe tip 3 initial.

*Combine Violet with Rose for violet shown.

d send a letter!

PANS
Round Pops Cookie Pan, Cookie Sheet, Cooling Grid

TIPS
2, 3, 4

COLORS*
Sky Blue, Golden Yellow, Black

RECIPES
Vanilla Sugar Cookies on a Stick, Color Flow Icing, p. 7

ALSO
101 Cookie Cutters Set (medium round), Cake Circle, 6 in. Cookie Treat Sticks, Parchment Paper; knife, ruler

INSTRUCTIONS
In advance: Make dots. For each pop, pipe twenty ¼ in. diameter tip 3 dots on parchment-covered cake circle. Make extras to allow for breakage. Let dry overnight.

Bake and cool cookies with sticks. Set on cooling grid over parchment-covered cookie sheet. Pour on thinned blue icing; tap to settle then let dry on parchment-covered surface. Set medium round cutter in center of cookie; score around inside edge with knife. Use full-strength pale yellow icing to pipe tip 2 outline; flow in with thinned icing. Let dry. Use icing to attach dots, about ¼ in. apart. Pipe tip 4 initial with full-strength icing.

*Combine Sky Blue with Golden Yellow for blue shown. Combine Black with Golden Yellow for gray shown.

Wilt

 **ode to olives**

PAN
9 x 13 x 2 in. Sheet

TIP
16

COLORS*
Christmas Red, Red-Red

FONDANT
White Ready-To-Use Rolled Fondant (¼ oz. per treat), Rolling Pin, Roll & Cut Mat

CANDY
Green, White Candy Melts, Primary (yellow, red) Candy Color Set, Chocolate Pro Melting Pot

RECIPES
Favorite Cake Ball Pops, Buttercream Icing, p. 7

ALSO
Pops Decorating Stand, 6 in. Lollipop Sticks; paring knife

INSTRUCTIONS
Prepare medium cake balls. Roll into olive shape. Insert wide end of tip 16 into larger side of olive, ⅜ in. deep, to make opening for pimiento. Use paring knife to trim out opening. Insert stick following pops recipe (p. 7); chill. Dip into melted candy. Place in Pops Decorating Stand. Chill until firm. For pimientos, roll out red fondant ⅛ in. thick. Cut ½ x ¾ in. pieces and insert into openings.

*Combine melted green candy with white candy, yellow and red candy colors for olive shade shown. Combine Christmas Red with Red-Red for red fondant shown.

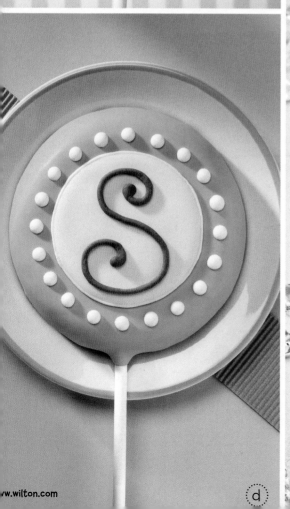

c brushed brilliance

PANS
Blossom Pops Cookie Pan, Cookie Sheet, Cooling Grid

TIPS
2, 3, 4

COLORS*
Rose, Sky Blue, Violet

RECIPES
Vanilla Sugar Cookies on a Stick, Royal Icing, p. 7

ALSO
White Pearl Dust, Imitation Clear Vanilla Extract, Meringue Powder, Brush Set, Parchment Paper, 8 in. Cookie Treat Sticks; knife, ruler, ¼ in. wide ribbon (14 in. per treat)

INSTRUCTIONS
In advance: Prepare dough and press into pops cavities with sticks. Bake and cool. Set on cooling grid set over parchment-covered cookie sheet. Reserve ½ cup white royal icing. Thin royal icing and tint. Pour over cookies to cover. Let dry overnight.

Decorate 1 petal at a time using slightly thinned icing. Outline petal using a zigzag motion; immediately brush icing toward center using square tipped brush. Use tip 4 for outside petals, tip 3 for middle petal and tip 2 for center petals. Finish with a tip 2 swirl in center. Let dry. Paint Pearl Dust/vanilla mixture over petal design. Tie on ribbon.

*Combine Violet with Rose for violet shown.

a flashy flowers

PANS
Blossom Pops Cookie Pan, Cookie Sheet, Cooling Grid

TIP
2

COLOR
Rose

FONDANT
White Ready-To-Use Rolled Fondant (½ oz. per treat), 9 in. Rolling Pin, Roll & Cut Mat, Brush Set, Gum-Tex

RECIPES
Vanilla Sugar Cookies on a Stick, Royal Icing, p. 7

ALSO
Flower Plastic Cutter, Pink Sugar Pearls, Pink Colored Sugar, White Sparkling Sugar, Meringue Powder, 8 in. Cookie Treat Sticks, Spatula; knife, ruler, ⅛ in. wide ribbon (12 in. per treat)

INSTRUCTIONS
In advance: Make fondant petals. Tint fondant and add Gum-Tex (½ tsp. for each 6 oz. of fondant). Roll out ⅛ in. thick. Cut using flower cutter. Use knife to cut into separate petals 1½ in. long. Let dry. Roll white fondant into ½ in. diameter ball; flatten. Brush with damp brush and sprinkle with white Sparkling Sugar. Let dry.

Prepare dough and press into pops cavities with sticks. Bake and cool. Spatula ice tops using full-strength pink royal icing; immediately sprinkle on pink colored sugar. Assemble using dots of icing. Roll ½ in. thick balls of fondant to angle petals. Attach fondant balls, petals and centers to cookie with icing. Attach Sugar Pearls with tip 2 icing dots. Let dry. Tie on ribbon.

b topiary treats

PAN
9 x 13 x 2 in. Sheet

TIP
349

COLORS*
Rose, Violet, Lemon Yellow, Moss Green

FONDANT
White Ready-To-Use Rolled Fondant (1 oz. per treat), 9 in. Rolling Pin, Roll & Cut Mat, Brush Set, Flower Cut-Outs, Fondant Shaping Foam, 10 Pc. Fondant/Gum Paste Tool Set

CANDY
White Candy Melts, Chocolate Pro Melting Pot

RECIPES
Favorite Cake Ball Pops, Buttercream Icing, p. 7

ALSO
White Sugar Pearls, Pops Decorating Stand, 6 in. Cookie Treat Sticks, Disposable Decorating Bags, Piping Gel, Light Green Colored Sugar; knife, ruler, ⅛ in. wide ribbon (14 in. per treat), vase

INSTRUCTIONS
In advance: Make flowers. Tint 1 oz. fondant per treat. Roll out 1/16 in. thick. Use smallest Cut-Out to cut about 35 flowers per treat. Set on thick foam and cup centers using dogbone tool from set. Let dry overnight. Attach Sugar Pearl center using dot of Piping Gel.

Prepare small cake balls and insert sticks following recipe. Chill. Dip in melted candy. Place in Decorating Stand until set. Attach flowers using melted candy. Pipe tip 349 buttercream leaves. Tie on ribbon. Fill vase with colored sugar; insert pop.

*Combine Violet with Rose for violet shown.

Wilt

d garden party pops

PANS
9 x 13 x 2 in. Sheet; Cookie Sheet; Cooling Grid

TIP
352

COLORS
Rose, Leaf Green

FONDANT
White Ready-To-Use Rolled Fondant (½ oz. per treat), 9 in. Rolling Pin; Roll & Cut Mat, Brush Set, Flower Cut-Outs, 10 Pc. Fondant/Gum Paste Tool Set, Fondant Shaping Foam

CANDY
White Candy Melts, Garden (pink) Candy Color Set

RECIPES
Favorite Cake Ball Pops, Buttercream Icing, p. 7

ALSO
Pops Doilies, White Sugar Pearls, Pops Decorating Stand, 8 in. Cookie Treat Sticks, Piping Gel, Cake Boards, Parchment Triangles, Parchment Paper; ¼ in. wide ribbon (12 in. lengths), knife

INSTRUCTIONS
In advance: Tint fondant 3 shades of rose. Roll out 1/16 in. thick. For each pop, cut 10 flowers in each shade using smallest Cut-Out. Place on thick foam and cup centers using small dogbone tool. Let dry on parchment. Attach Sugar Pearl center with Piping Gel.

Prepare large cake balls and cut in half. Chill. Tint candy pink. Ice flat bottoms with melted candy. Let set on parchment-covered surface. Set candy-side down on cooling grid over parchment-lined cookie sheet. Pour on melted candy to cover. Tap to settle; chill until firm. Use knife tip to poke hole in bottom. Insert stick and secure with melted candy. Slide on doily. Attach flowers using melted candy in cut parchment bag. Pipe tip 352 buttercream leaves. Tie a ribbon bow. Attach to doily with melted candy.

e forget-me-not pops

PAN
9 x 13 x 2 in. Sheet

TIP
3

COLORS*
Lemon Yellow, Golden Yellow, Royal Blue, Violet, Rose

FONDANT
White Ready-To-Use Rolled Fondant (¼ oz. per treat), 9 in. Rolling Pin, Roll & Cut Mat, Brush Set, Flower Cut-Outs

CANDY
Light Cocoa Candy Melts, Chocolate Pro Melting Pot

RECIPES
Favorite Cake Ball Pops, Buttercream Icing, p. 7

ALSO
Pops Decorating Stand, 8 in. Cookie Treat Sticks; knife, ruler

INSTRUCTIONS
Prepare large cake balls and insert sticks following recipe. Chill. Dip in melted candy. Place in Decorating Stand; chill until firm. For flowers, tint fondant and roll out 1/8 in. thick. Cut using medium Cut-Out. Use knife to cut deeper petals. Attach to pop using melted candy. Pipe tip 3 icing swirl center.

*Combine Violet with Rose for violet shown. Combine Lemon Yellow with Golden Yellow for yellow shown

f dining with daisy

PANS
9 x 5 in. Loaf, Cookie Sheet, Cooling Grid

CANDY
White Candy Melts; Garden (pink) Candy Color Set

ALSO
Nesting Blossom Cookie Cutter (3rd from smallest used), Jumbo Confetti Sprinkles, 6 in. Cookie Treat Sticks, 12 in. Disposable Decorating Bags, Parchment Paper; green curling ribbon, green construction paper, scissors, hole punch

INSTRUCTIONS
Bake and cool cake using a firm-textured batter like pound cake. Cut into ½ in. slices. Using 3rd smallest blossom cutter, cut out shapes. Ice bottoms with melted candy. Chill. Insert sticks following pops recipe (p. 7). Set on cooling grid over parchment-covered cookie sheet. Cover with melted pink candy; tap to settle and chill until firm. Use melted pink candy in cut disposable bag to outline petals. Place jumbo confetti in center of flower. Chill to set. Cut paper leaf, punch hole and tie leaf to stick with ribbon.

a pastel pops pronto!

PAN
9 x 13 x 2 in. Sheet

CANDY
White Candy Melts, Primary (yellow, blue), Garden (pink, green) Candy Color Sets, Chocolate Pro Melting Pot

RECIPE
Favorite Cake Ball Pops, p. 7

ALSO
White Sparkling Sugar, Pops Decorating Stand, 11¾ in. Lollipop Sticks; knife

INSTRUCTIONS
Prepare small cake balls and insert sticks following recipe. Chill. Dip in melted, tinted candy. Immediately roll in sugar to coat bottom half. Place in Decorating Stand; chill until firm.

b triple dippers

PAN
9 x 13 x 2 in. Sheet

CANDY
White, Light Cocoa Candy Melts; Primary (blue, yellow), Garden (green, pink) Candy Color Sets, Chocolate Pro Melting Pot

RECIPE
Favorite Cake Ball Pops, p. 7

ALSO
Pops Decorating Stand, 6 in. Cookie Treat Sticks

INSTRUCTIONS
Prepare medium cake balls and insert sticks following recipe. Chill. Dip completely in melted white or cocoa candy. Place in Decorating Stand; chill until firm. Dip pops in candy tinted lighter shades, covering bottom ⅔. Chill until firm. Dip pops in candy tinted darker shades, covering bottom ⅓. Chill until firm.

c too marbleous for words

PAN
9 x 13 x 2 in. Sheet

CANDY
White, Light Cocoa Candy Melts, Primary (blue), Garden (green, pink) Candy Color Sets, Chocolate Pro Melting Pot

RECIPE
Favorite Cake Ball Pops, p. 7

ALSO
Pops Decorating Stand, 11¾ in. Lollipop Sticks

INSTRUCTIONS
Prepare small cake balls and insert sticks following recipe. Chill. Prepare ½ cup bowls of melted white and cocoa candy and smaller amounts of tinted candy. Add 1-2 tablespoons of tinted candy on top of white or cocoa candy. Dip and swirl pops to cover. Place in Decorating Stand; chill until firm.

a

b

c

Wilt

d pastels and pearls

PAN
9 x 13 x 2 in. Sheet

CANDY
White Candy Melts, Primary (blue, yellow), Garden (pink, green) Candy Color Sets; Chocolate Pro Melting Pot

RECIPE
Favorite Cake Ball Pops, p. 7

ALSO
White, Green, Pink, Yellow Sugar Pearls; Pops Decorating Stand, Parchment Triangles, 6 in. Cookie Treat Sticks; tweezers

INSTRUCTIONS
Prepare medium cake balls and insert sticks following recipe. Chill. Dip pops in melted candy; tap to settle. Place in Decorating Stand; chill until firm. Using same color melted candy in cut parchment bag, pipe top of pop; tap to smooth. Attach Sugar Pearls with tweezers. Chill until firm.

e imperial pops

PAN
9 x 13 x 2 in. Sheet

COLORS*
Rose, Royal Blue, Lemon Yellow, Golden Yellow, Kelly Green

FONDANT
White Ready-To-Use Rolled Fondant, 9 in. Rolling Pin, Brush Set, Roll & Cut Mat

RECIPE
Favorite Cake Ball Pops, p. 7

ALSO
Light Cocoa Candy Melts, White Sparkling Sugar, Pops Decorating Stand, 11¾ in. Lollipop Sticks, Chocolate Pro Melting Pot; knife, ruler, goblets

INSTRUCTIONS
Prepare small cake balls and insert sticks following recipe. Chill. Dip in melted candy. Place in Decorating Stand; chill until firm. Tint fondant (½ oz. per pop) and roll out 1/16 in. thick. Cut eight 2 x ⅛ in. wide strips per pop; attach using damp brush, trimming at bottom as needed. Let set. Brush strips with damp brush and sprinkle on sugar. Fill goblets with sugar; position pops.

*Combine Lemon Yellow with Golden Yellow for yellow shown.

For the do-it-yourself hostess, our monogrammed pop is one of the easiest and most impressive designs. Simply give your cake ball pop a quick dip in melted candy, chill and pipe the candy initial. It's letter-perfect!

a sparkle on a stick

PAN
9 x 13 x 2 in. Sheet

CANDY
White Candy Dips

RECIPE
Favorite Cake Ball Pops, p. 7

ALSO
Silver, Gold Pearlized Sugar; 6 in. Lollipop Sticks, Pops Decorating Stand

INSTRUCTIONS
Prepare small cake balls and insert sticks following recipe; chill. Dip pops in melted candy; immediately dip in Pearlized Sugars to cover completely. Place in Decorating Stand. Chill until firm.

b majestic monogram

PAN
9 x 13 x 2 in. Sheet

CANDY
White, Light Cocoa Candy Melts, Chocolate Pro Melting Pot

RECIPE
Favorite Cake Ball Pops, p. 7

ALSO
Parchment Triangles, Parchment Paper, 6 in. Cookie Treat Sticks, Pops Treat Bags, Cake Board

INSTRUCTIONS
Prepare large cake balls and insert sticks following recipe; chill. Dip pops in melted candy. Position pops on parchment-covered board. Chill until firm. Using melted candy in cut parchment bag, pipe initial in opposite color of pops; chill until firm.

c) cocoa kabobs

PAN
9 x 13 x 2 in. Sheet

CANDY
Light Cocoa, White Candy Melts, Chocolate Pro Melting Pot

RECIPE
Favorite Cake Ball Pops, p. 7

ALSO
Turtle Crunch, Cookies 'n Cream Crunch, Pops Decorating Stand, 11¾ in. Lollipop Sticks, 4 in. Lollipop Sticks, Parchment Triangles; toasted coconut, chopped nuts, mini chocolate chips, knife, ruler

INSTRUCTIONS
Prepare small and medium cake balls (2 of each size per kabob) and insert a 4 in. stick in each, following recipe. Chill. Dip in melted candy. Roll in various toppings. Place in Decorating Stand and let set. Use melted candy in cut parchment bag to pipe a candy ring about 4 in. from top on 11¾ in. sticks. Chill until firm then overpipe; let set. Twist balls off of 4 in. sticks and slide onto 11¾ in. sticks, alternating sizes. Secure top and bottom treats with melted candy.

d) sweet & salty

PAN
9 x 13 x 2 in. Sheet

CANDY
White, Light Cocoa Candy Melts, Chocolate Pro Melting Pot

RECIPE
Favorite Cake Ball Pops, p. 7

ALSO
Pops Decorating Stand, 6 in. Lollipop Sticks; chopped nuts (we used peanuts and pecans), knife, ruler

INSTRUCTIONS
Prepare small cake balls and insert sticks following recipe. Chill. Dip in melted candy. Then roll in nuts. Place in Decorating Stand and chill. Dip in melted candy. Chill until firm.

d)

The power of pops can't be contained! However, we can offer many great ways to present pops gifts that show off your delightful designs at their best. The Wilton boxes and bags shown here are ideal for adding your own special touches, including ribbon, colored paper and stickers. Find the complete selection of pops presentation products on page 111.

pops gift boxes

Windows let the sunny faces of your pops shine through! Just use your favorite stickers, curling ribbon and cardboard to set the scene. Create a merry gingerbread house, a bubbly aquarium, jolly circus train or build a party room for the birthday girl and all her friends. With our presentation packaging, it's easy to think outside the box!

pops flower pot kit

A garden of gifts can grow from this cool container! Arrange pops at various heights in the secure double-base insert, then use your own colorful paper and ribbon to decorate a fun custom design to fit the occasion. Whether you're planting pops with petals or space faces on sticks, this container will make your treats look terrific. Or, for a simple presentation, wrap up pops with the bag, ribbon and tag included.

pops favor bags

Single pops make the perfect favor, stocking stuffer or gift topper—and there's no better way to present them than with these see-through bags. Gather the bag around your pop, then tie on the included ribbon along with your own gift tag.

pops products

Ready to create fun pops on a stick for family and friends? From everyday treats to special occasion desserts, the pops you create will bring ooohs and aaahs to your celebration. Just choose from this great selection of Wilton pops products, and you will be ready to bake, decorate and present the best pops treats imaginable!

pops baking preparation

Baking prep has never been easier with this high-quality selection of Wilton Better Baking Tools—essential for those perfect results you desire!

Silicone Spoon Scraper
One tool is all you need for scooping, scraping and mixing. Flexible pointed tip gets into hard-to-reach corners. Patent No. D584,927. 11 in. long.
2103-328

Silicone Universal Scraper
Flat, flexible end for pans and bowls, small rounded end for jars. Patent No. D586,630. 11 in. long.
2103-327

Silicone Stand Mixer Scraper
Angled neck and unique flexible silicone head easily mix dough back into bottom of bowl with mixer attachment in place. Patent No. D587,537. 11 in. long.
2103-329

Cyclone Whisk
Center spiral whips up more air! Patent No. D582,223.
2103-317

Tilt-N-Mix 3 Pc. Bowl Set
Bowls tip at an angle without falling over—makes mixing easy! Includes 1.5, 3 and 5 quart bowls. Set/3
2103-306

Scoop-It Measuring Tools
Unique spade shaped design. Snap-on ring gives easy access to each cup or spoon.

Cups
Includes 1 cup, ½ cup, ⅓ cup, ¼ cup. Patent No. D582,297. Set/4
2103-324

Spoons
Includes 1 tablespoon, 1 teaspoon, ½ teaspoon, ¼ teaspoon, ⅛ teaspoon. Patent No. D582,298. Set/5
2103-325

Liquid Measuring Cups
Unique step design lets you read measurements from above. Patent Pending.
2 Cup 2103-334
4 Cup 2103-335

pops baking and shaping

Wilton has the best products to help you bake and shape fun pops treats. You'll love this selection of non-stick, aluminum and silicone bakeware—designed for even heating and easy clean-up too. Dowel rods and pillars make it easy to shape uniform pop cylinders for designs like candles and crayons.

non-stick bakeware

Jelly Roll Pans
Small
13.25 x 9.25 x .6 in.
2105-966
Medium
15.25 x 10.25 x .75 in.
2105-967
Large
17.25 x 11.5 x 1 in.
2105-968

Oblong Cake Pan
13 x 9 x 2 in.
2105-961

Jumbo Air Insulated Cookie Sheet
18 x 14 in.
2105-978

Large Air Insulated Cookie Sheet
16 x 14 in.
2105-977

aluminum bakeware

3-D Mini Bear Pan
2-piece pan bakes cakes
2.25 x 2.25 x 1.25 in.
2105-0545

Round Pops Cookie Pan
Cavities: 4.25 x .5 in.
2105-0536

Heart Pops Cookie Pan
Cavities: 4.25 x 4 x .5 in.
2105-0537

Flower Pops Cookie Pan
Cavities: 4.25 x 4 x .5 in.
2105-0539

Star Pops Cookie Pan
Cavities: 4.25 x 4 x .5 in.
2105-0538

Insulated Sheet
Two quality aluminum layers sandwich an insulating layer of air for perfect browning without burning.
14 x 16 in.
2105-2644

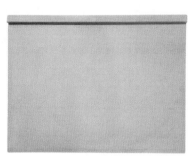

Jumbo Sheet
Extra-thick construction heats evenly for perfectly browned bottoms.
14 x 20 in.
2105-6213

Jelly Roll and Cookie Pan
Wilton pans are 1 in. deep for fuller-looking desserts.

10.5 x 15.5 x 1 in.
2105-1269

12 x 18 x 1 in.
2105-4854

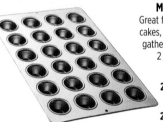

Mini Muffin
Great for mini cheese-cakes, brunches, large gatherings. Cups are 2 in. x .75 in.

12 Cup
2105-2125

24 Cup
2105-9313

9 x 5 in. Loaf
Favorite size for homemade breads and cakes.
2105-3688

Sheet Pans

9 x 13 x 2 in.
2105-1308

11 x 15 x 2 in.
2105-158

12 x 18 x 2 in.
2105-182

silicone bakeware

Heart Pops Mold
dividual cavities are 2 x 5 x .75 in. deep.
2105-0588

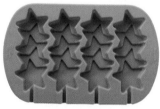

Star Pops Mold
Individual cavities are 2.25 x 5 x .5 in. deep.
2105-0546

Round Brownie Pops Mold
One 8 x 8 in. size brownie mix makes 24 brownies. Individual cavities are 1.75 x 1.75 x 1.75 in. deep.
2105-4925

Silicone Baking Mat
Line cookie sheets—protects against burned bottoms and cleans up with ease! Or, use as a pastry mat. 10 x 15 in.
2105-4808

Boy Mold
One mix makes approximately 80 gingerbread boys. 24 cavities, each 1.75 x 1.6 x .75 in. deep.
2105-0553

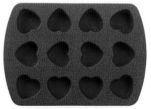

Petite Hearts Mold
1.5 x 1.5 x 1 in. deep.
2105-4860

Hearts Mold
Individual cavities are 2.5 x 2.5 x 1.5 in. deep.
2105-4824

shaping tools

Plastic Dowel Rods
Length: 12.25 in. Diam.: .75 in. Pk./4.
399-801

"Hidden" Pillars
Trimmable, hollow plastic.
6 in. high. Pk./4.
303-8

POPS! sweets on a stick!

baking accessories

Cake Release

Another step-saving Wilton idea! No need to grease and flour your baking pan—Cake Release coats in one step. Simply spread Cake Release lightly on pan bottom and sides with a pastry brush and add batter. Cakes release perfectly every time without crumbs, giving you the ideal surface for decorating. In convenient dispensing bottle. 8 oz. Certified Kosher.
702-6016

Bake Easy! Non-Stick Spray

This convenient non-stick spray helps your baked goods release perfectly. Just a light, even coating does the job. Versatile for all types of baking and cooking. 6 oz.
702-6018

Flavors

Delicious extracts add concentrated flavor. Use clear extracts to mix with Pearl Dust and paint your pops! Certified Kosher.

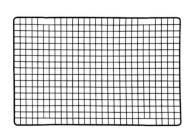

Pure Vanilla Extract

Unmatched flavor and aroma of pure vanilla enhances cookies, cakes, puddings, icings, custards and more. 4 fl. oz.
604-2270

Imitation Clear Vanilla Extract
2 fl. oz. 604-2237
8 fl. oz. 604-2269

Imitation Clear Almond Extract
2 fl. oz. 604-2126

Chrome Cooling Grids

Sturdy design will never rust.

14.5 x 20 in.
2305-129

13 in. Round
2305-130

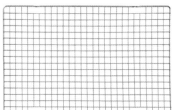

Non-Stick Cooling Grids

10 x 16 in. Rectangle
2305-228

14.5 x 20 in. Rectangle
2305-229

13 in. Round
2305-230

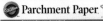

Non-Stick Parchment Paper

Use Wilton silicone-treated non-stick parchment to line baking pans and cookie sheets—a non-fat alternative that saves cleanup time. Double roll is 41 square feet, 15 in. wide. Certified Kosher.
415-680

---

cutters

Wilton has the cutter shapes and styles you want that create the distinctive cookie pops everyone love. Check out all the fun shapes—from seasonal to special everyday cutters—for all your celebrations.

Comfort-Grip Cutters

Easy-grip stainless steel cutters with extra-deep sides are perfect for cutting brownies and other favorite foods into spectacular shapes. Each approximately 4 x 4 x 1.75 in.

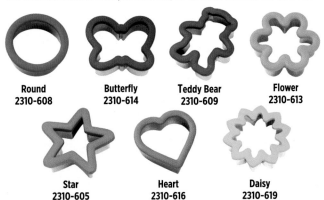

Round
2310-608

Butterfly
2310-614

Teddy Bear
2310-609

Flower
2310-613

Star
2310-605

Heart
2310-616

Daisy
2310-619

Metal Cutter Sets

Multi-piece sets are designed in popular themes for kids and adults. Built to last, they cut cleanly and release easily.

Football
Pennant, football, jersey, and helmet. Each approx. 3 in. Set/4.
2308-1263

Nesting From The Heart
Two crinkled, two smooth. Largest is approx. 5 in. Set/4
2308-1203

9 Pc. Leaves and Acorns Nesting Metal Cutter Set
Set of 9 includes graduated acorns, oak and maple leaves (3 each). 1.75 to 3.75 in. Set/9
2308-2000

3 Pc. Trees Cutter Set
Set of 3 includes triangle tree, start tree and classic fi each approx. 3 in Coated metal. Set/
2308-1103

Metal Cookie Cutters

Metal cutters from Wilton are built to last through years of cookie making; they cut cleanly and release with ease. Each shape is approximately 3 in.

Star
2308-1008

Daisy
2308-1007

Heart
2308-1003

Butterfly
2308-1015

Circle
2308-1010

Oak Leaf
2308-1013

Gingerbread Boy
2308-1002

Plastic Nesting Cutter Sets

Your favorites in child-safe, graduated shapes. Discover all the fun ways to use our cutters—for bread shapes, stencils, sun catchers and so much more.

Heart
1.5 to 4.2 in. Set/6.
2304-115

Star
1.6 to 4.6 in. Set/6.
2304-111

Blossom
1.2 to 4.5 in. Set/6.
2304-116

Cookie Press

Making traditional spritz cookies has never been so easy! Cookie P Ultra II is designed to be the easiest to fill, most comfortable pres you've ever used. With 12 terrific shapes, plus 4 fun mini cookie designs, your holiday cookie baskets will be more festive than ever Includes complete instructions and delicious recipes. Set/17
2104-4018

Twelve Disks in Festive Shapes

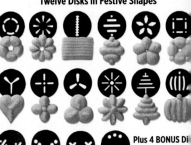

Plus 4 BONUS Di For Mini Cookie

Wilt

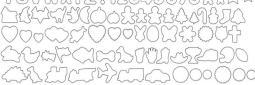

Animal Pals 50-Piece Cutter Set
Shapes include fish, dog, cat, birds, butterflies, reptiles and more. Average cutter size approx. 3.5 x 3.5 in. Set/50.
2304-1055

101 Cookie Cutters Set
Make cookies featuring popular holiday and theme shapes. Average cutter size approx. 3.5 x 3.5 in. Recipe included. Plastic. Set/101
2304-1050

pops candy and tools
Let Wilton show you how easy pop making can be! Use Candy Melts and colors, specially designed melting tools and sturdy sticks to dip and create amazing pops and treats.

Chocolate Pro Melting Pot
- The fast and easy way to melt chocolate and Candy Melts!
- Melting base stays cool to the touch
- Removeable non-stick Melting Pot holds 2½ cups
- Easy-pour spout
- Non-skid feet keep Chocolate Pro steady
- It's the fast and fun way to mold candies like a pro

With the Chocolate Pro, you'll be able to mold lollipops and fancy dipped-center candies. Serve dipped desserts like brownie pops, fruit, cake, cookies and fondue. Add the great taste of chocolate to potato chips and pretzels. Create flavored chocolate sauces for ice cream or silky ganache glaze to pour over cakes. 120 volts. CUL Listed.
2104-9004

Melting Cups
Cups are great for melting colors separately. Use them like an art palette for painting colors. Holds heat up to ½ hour. Includes 6 cups (2 x 1.5 in. deep) and 6 decorating brushes. Set/12.
1904-1067

Melting Bowls
Ideal for filling all types of Wilton molds. Take them to the table for easy dipping. Holds heat up to 1 hour. Two, 4 x 3.5 in. deep. Set/2.
1904-1076

Lollipop Sticks
Sturdy paper sticks in 4 sizes. Not for oven use.

4 in. Pk./50.
1912-1006

6 in. Pk./35.
1912-1007

8 in. Pk./25.
1912-9320

11¾ in. Pk./20.
1912-1212

Cookie Treat Sticks
For fun cookie pops.

6 in. Pk./20.
1912-9319

8 in. Pk./20.
1912-9318

Candy Melts
Versatile, creamy, easy-to-melt wafers are ideal for dipping and drizzling pops and mini treats. Choose your favorite from a rainbow of colors! Light and Dark Cocoa are all natural cocoa flavor; colors are artificially vanilla flavored. All come in 14 oz. bags, except Colorburst Primary and Pastel, Spooky Green and Midnight Black, which are 10 oz. bags. Certified Kosher Dairy.

Dark Cocoa
1911-358

Light Cocoa
1911-544

Dark Cocoa Mint
1911-1920

Peanut Butter
1911-481

Green
1911-405

White
1911-498

Blue
1911-448

Yellow
1911-463

Orange
1911-1631

Red
1911-499

Pink
1911-447

Lavender
1911-403

Colorburst Brights
10 oz.
1911-491

Colorburst Pastel
10 oz.
1911-490

Spooky Green
10 oz.
1911-488

Midnight Black
10 oz.
1911-489

Midnight Black and Spooky Green Available Seasonally Only

Candy Dips
Designed for fun, easy dipping of pops, treats, fruit, cookies and more with little prep. Quick melting right in the container using your microwave. 10 oz. Certified Kosher Dairy.

Light Cocoa 1911-511

White 1911-510

Garden Candy Color Set
Create pretty pastel colors! Concentrated oil-based colors blend easily with Candy Melts. Includes Pink, Green, Violet and Black in .25 oz. jars. Certified Kosher.
1913-1298 Set/4

Primary Candy Color Set
Concentrated oil-based colors blend easily with Candy Melts. Includes Yellow, Orange, Red and Blue in .25 oz. jars. Certified Kosher.
1913-1299 Set/4

pops decorating essentials

It is simple to create amazing pops and treat designs when you have the right tools! Take a look at this selection of time-saving tools that will make your pop and treat making so much easier!

Pops Decorating Stand

Securely holds your pops upright as you decorate—great when making multiples of any design. It's the ideal way to let the candy set on your pops undisturbed. Holds up to 44 pops. 12 in. dia. X 1.75 in. high.
1512-136

Brush Set

Fine-bristle brushes in three tip designs (round, square and bevel), help you achieve different painted effects. Set/3
1907-1207

Decorator Brush Set

Plastic, durable bristles, easy-to-hold handle. Set/3.
2104-9355

Candy Melting Plate

Microwave-melt up to 11 Candy Melts colors at one time with less mess! Plastic with non-slip grip edge. Includes decorating brush.
1904-8016

White Baking Cups

Standard Pk./75.
415-2505

Mini Pk./100.
415-2507

Decorating Bags

All decorating bags are not the same! Wilton bags are tested to be the best. They simply feel better in your hand—soft and strong to provide decorating performance you can count on. From pure parchment triangles to our convenient Disposable, Wilton bags are made to our strict specifications for consistent quality.

Parchment Triangles

Authentic parchment paper is the professional's choice for convenience and quick bag preparation. Make use-and-toss decorating bags ideal for small amounts of icing or brush striping. Excellent wet strength for candy or a variety of icings. Also great for smoothing iced cakes and transferring patterns. 15 in. Pk./100
2104-1508

Icing Spatulas

Contoured handle with finger pad provides an excellent grip and superior control.

Straight
Great for spreading and smoothing fillings, all-around kitchen use.
9 in. **409-6006**
11 in. **409-6018**
15 in. **409-6030**

Angled
Ideal angle for smoothing cake sides and spreading fillings.
9 in. **409-6012**
13 in. **409-6024**
15 in. **409-6036**

Tapered
Easily ices hard-to-reach spots on your cake. 9 in.
409-6003

9 in. Fondant Roller

Roll to the perfect ⅛ or 1/16 in. height used for cutting many fondant decorations, using the slide-on guide rings. Easy to handle—just the right size for preparing small amounts of fondant to place on your cake. 9 x 1 in. diameter. Includes ⅛ and 1/16 in. rings.
1907-1205

Roll & Cut Mat

For precise measuring, rolling and cutting of fondant or dough. Pre-marked circles for exact sizing. Square grid helps you cut precise strips. Non-stick surface for easy release. 20 in. square with circles from 3 in. to 19 in. diam.
409-412

Wave Flower Former Set

Use this convenient connecting platform to dry flowers, leaves and other decorations in royal icing, gum paste or fondant. 14.5 x 9 in. assembled. Patent pending. Set/2.
1907-1320

Flower Forming Cups

Includes 2.5 and 3 in. diameter cups for drying everything from simple blossoms and briar roses to large daisies. Set/6.
1907-118

Fondant Shaping Foam

Thick and thin squares are the ideal surface for shaping flowers, leaves and other fondant or gum paste cutouts. Thin: 4 x 4 x .2 in. Thick: 4 x 4 x 1 in. Set/2.
1907-9704

Dusting Pouches

Gathering cord closes pouch securely—just tap lightly on the pouch to sprinkle. 7 in. diameter. Pk./4.
417-106

Disposable Decorating Bags

Wilton's strict testing standards ensure the highest quality disposable bags you can buy. Our proprietary blend of materials helps Wilton bags feel more comfortable and outperform competitive bags. They can be used with or without a coupler and work great for microwave-melting and piping of Candy Melts. Fits standard tips and couplers. Just use, then toss! Instructions included.
12 in. Pk./12 **2104-358**
12 in. Pk./24 **2104-1358**
16 in. Pk./12 **2104-1357**

10-Pc. Fondant/Gum Paste Tool Set

Convenient case keeps the collection organized and handy. Includes large/small veining tool, shell tool/ knife, large/small dogbone tool, serrated quilting/cutting wheel, umbrella tool with 5 and 6 divisions, scriber/cone tool, large/small ball tool, palette knife and modeling sticks #1 and #2. Set/10.
1907-1107

Cake Circles

Corrugated cardboard for strength and stability.
6 in. diameter Pk./10 **2104-64**
8 in. diameter Pk./12 **2104-80**
10 in. diameter Pk./12 **2104-102**
12 in. diameter Pk./8 **2104-129**
14 in. diameter Pk./6 **2104-145**
16 in. diameter Pk./6 **2104-160**

Fanci-Foil Wrap

Serving side has a grease-resistant surface. Continuous roll: 20 in. x 15 ft.
White 804-191
Gold 804-183
Silver 804-167

Wilton

Decorator Icing
eal stiff consistency for making roses and flowers th upright petals. One 16 oz. can covers two 8 or 9 in. layers or one 9 x 13 in. cake. 16 oz. can.
White 710-118
Chocolate 710-119

Color Flow Mix
Create dimensional flow-in designs for your cake. Just add water and confectioners' sugar. 4 oz. can makes ten 1½ cup batches. Certified Kosher.
701-47

Piping Gel
Pipe messages and designs or glaze cakes before icing. Use clear or tint with icing color. 10 oz. Certified Kosher.
704-105

Gum-Tex
Makes fondant and gum paste pliable, elastic, easy to shape. Plastic resealable lid. 6 oz. Certified Kosher.
707-117

Meringue Powder
Primary ingredient for royal icing. Stabilizes buttercream, adds body to boiled icing and meringue. Replaces egg whites in many recipes. Resealable top opens for easy measuring. 4 oz. can makes 5 recipes of royal icing; 8 oz. can makes 10 recipes. 16 oz. can makes 20 recipes. Certified Kosher.
4 oz. 702-6007
8 oz. 702-6015
16 oz. 702-6004

pops decorations

Add some fun with sprinkles, sugars, sparkles and crunches! Distinctive shapes, a variety of textures, and a rainbow of colors add excitement to all your treats on sticks, cake balls, cupcakes, cookies, treats and more.

Sprinkle Set
Use for people faces. Diamonds, circles and jimmies. 3.74 oz. total wt.
710-056

Sprinkle Set
Use for animal faces. Jimmies, triangles, and ovals. 3.74 oz. total wt.
710-055

Colored Sugar
Extra-fine sugar is excellent for filling in brightly colored designs on pops, brownies, cakes, cupcakes and cookies. 3.25 oz. bottle. Certified Kosher.

Blue 710-750	**Pink** 710-756	**Red** 710-766
Yellow 710-754	**Light Green** 710-752	**Dark Green** 710-764
Lavender 710-758	**Orange** 710-759	**Black** 710-762

Sparkling Sugar
asy-pour sugars have a coarse texture and rilliant sparkle. 8 oz. bottle. Certified Kosher.

Blue 710-039	**Pink** 710-038
Yellow 710-036	**White** 710-992

Crunches
Add exciting color, taste and texture in an stant! Perfect flavor combinations for brown-es; great on ice cream, too. Certified Kosher.

ookies 'N Cream 5 oz. bottle **710-9702**

Rainbow Chip 5.25 oz. bottle Certified Kosher dairy. **710-9704**

Turtle 5 oz. bottle **710-9703**

Jumbo Sprinkles
Bold shapes in bright colors add big impact to pops, treats and special designs. Jumbo decorations are the perfect way to finish your celebration pops, treats, cupcakes, cookies and cakes. Certified Kosher.

Jumbo Confetti 3.25 oz. bottle **710-029**

Jumbo Daisies 3.25 oz. bottle **710-028**

Jumbo Hearts 3.25 oz. bottle **710-032**

Jumbo Stars 3.25 oz. bottle **710-026**

Jumbo Rainbow Nonpareils 4.8 oz. bottle **710-033**

6-Mix Assortments
They're so convenient! Assorted fun shapes in an easy-pour flip-top bottle. Top pops, cupcakes, ice cream and other goodies. Certified Kosher.

Flowerful Medley Includes Confetti, Colorful Leaves, Daisies, Pastel Hearts, Wild Flowers, Butterflies. 2.2 oz. total. **710-4122**

Jimmies Includes Pink, Orange, Green, Red, Yellow, Blue. 2.52 oz. total. **710-4127**

Shaped Sprinkles
Pour on the fun! Great shapes and colors add a dash of excitement to pops, brownies, cakes, cupcakes, ice cream and more. Certified Kosher.

Rainbow Jimmies 2.5 oz. bottle **710-776**

Chocolate Jimmies 2.5 oz. bottle **710-774**

Rainbow Nonpareils 3 oz. bottle **710-772**

White Nonpareils 3 oz. bottle **710-773**

Cinnamon Drops 3 oz. **710-769**

Cake Sparkles
Add shimmering color to pops, brownies cakes, cupcakes, cookies and ice cream! Brilliant edible glitter in a great variety of colors, great for stenciling, highlighting messages, snow scenes. .25 oz. Certified Kosher.

| **Silver** 03-1285 | **White** 703-1290 | **Yellow** 703-1272 | **Purple** 703-1266 | **Blue** 703-1314 | **Red** 703-1284 | **Green** 703-1278 | **Pink** 703-1260 | **Orange** 703-1308 | **Black** 703-1302 |

Pearlized Sprinkles

Create a color sensation on your pops, cakes and cupcakes! Add the soft, shimmering look of Sugar Pearls in 5 glistening shades. Or, shake on the sparkle with dazzling Pearlized Sugars and Jimmies! Certified Kosher.

Sugar Pearls
5 oz.
710-044

 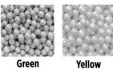 

| Green Sugar Pearls 5 oz. 710-1130 | Yellow Sugar Pearls 5 oz. 710-1131 | Pink Sugar Pearls 5 oz. 710-1132 | Blue Sugar Pearls 5 oz. 710-1133 |

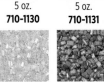 

| Pearlized Sugar 5.25 oz. 710-043 | Gold Pearlized Sugar 5.25 oz. 710-041 | Silver Pearlized Sugar 5.25 oz. 710-042 | Ruby Pearlized Sugar 5.25 oz. 710-046 |

| Sapphire Pearlized Sugar 5.25 oz. 710-047 | Emerald Pearlized Sugar 5.25 oz. 710-048 | Pearlized Jimmies 4.5 oz. 710-045 |

White Ready-To-Use Rolled Fondant

Fondant has never been more convenient and easy to use for decorating! With Wilton Ready-To-Use Rolled Fondant, there's no mess, no guesswork. The 24 oz. (1.5 Lb.) package covers an 8 in. 2-layer cake plus decorations; the 80 oz. (5 Lb.) package covers a 2-layer 6 in., 8 in. and 10 in. round tiered cake plus decorations. Pure white. Certified Kosher.

24 oz. (1.5 Lb.) Pk.
710-2076

Color Fondant Multi Packs

Convenient four-pouch assortments are perfect for multicolored flowers and borders. Each 17.6 oz. package contains four 4.4 oz. packs. Certified Kosher.

Primary Colors
Green, Red, Yellow, Blue
710-445

Neon Colors
Purple, Orange, Yellow, Pink
710-446

Pastel Colors
Blue, Yellow, Pink, Green
710-447

Natural Colors
Light Brown, Dark Brown, Pink, Black
710-448

Pearl Dust

Easy to use, just brush onto your decoration with a soft artist brush. Or, to paint decorations, pour a small amount of lemon extract; stir in Pearl Dust and brush onto your decoration. Edible; Certified Kosher (except Orchid Pink and Lilac Purple). .05 oz. bottle.

| Leaf Green 703-215 | Lilac Purple 703-221 | Sapphire Blue 703-222 | Ruby Red 703-223 | Gold 703-216 |

| Yellow 703-213 | Bronze 703-214 | Orchid Pink 703-217 | Silver 703-218 | White 703-219 |

Icing Color

Easy-mixing colors are great for tinting fondant, icings, cookie dough and more! Produce deep, rich color with just a small amount using this fast-mixing gel. The Wilton exclusive concentrated gel formula was developed to help decorators achieve the exact shade desired without changing icing consistency. An unmatched color selection makes it easy for you to achieve virtually any shade. Single Bottles 1 oz. Certified Kosher.

*Note: Large amount of these colors may affect icng taste.

When using black, start with chocolate icing to limit the amount of color used.

‡Daffodil Yellow is an all-natural color. It does not contain Yellow #5. The color remains very pale.

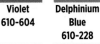

Ivory 610-208	Daffodil Yellow‡ 610-175	Buttercup Yellow 610-216	Golden Yellow 610-159
Lemon Yellow 610-108	Copper 610-450	Creamy Peach 610-210	Rose Petal Pink 610-410
Terra Cotta 610-206	Orange 610-205	Red (no-taste) 610-998	Christmas Red* 610-302
Red-Red* 610-906	Rose 610-401	Burgundy 610-698	Pink 610-256
Violet 610-604	Delphinium Blue 610-228	Cornflower Blue 610-710	Royal Blue 610-655
Sky Blue 610-700	Teal 610-207	Kelly Green 610-752	Leaf Green 610-809
Moss Green 610-851	Juniper Green 610-234	Brown 610-507	Black* 610-981

Cut-Outs

With Cut-Outs, it's easy to make fun 3-D shapes to dress up your pops, cakes and cupcakes. Just roll out fondant and/or gum paste, press down with Cut-Out and lift away. Remove shapes with a small spatula. Stainless steel (except for plastic Daisy) shapes range from .6 in. to 2.5 in.

**A B C D E F G
H I J K L M N
O P Q R S T U
V W X Y Z 0 1
2 3 4 5 6 7 8 9**

Alphabet/Number
.75 to .875 in. Set/37.
417-442

FoodWriter Edible Color Markers

Use like ink markers to add fun and dazzling color to counte[l] foods. Kids love 'em! Decorate o[n] fondant, color flow, Wilton Cook[ie] Icing, royal icing, even directly o[n] cookies. Brighten everyday food[s] like toaster pastries, cheese, fru[it] slices, bread and more. Each se[t] includes five .07 oz. FoodWriter[™] markers. Certified Kosher.

| Yellow | Green |
| Red | Blue |

Black

FINE TIP
BOLD TIP

Primary Color Sets
Fine Tip Set/5. 609-100
Bold Tip Set/5. 609-115

Truffles Candy Mold
1 design, 14 cavities.
2115-1521

Cordial Cups Candy Mold
1 design, 6 cavities.
2115-1535

Girl Power 2 Pack Candy Mold
10 designs, 10 cavities. Pk./2.
2115-1604

| Oval .625 to 2.25 in. Set/3. 417-438 | Round .75 to 2.25 in. Set/3. 417-432 | Square .625 to 2.25 in. Set/3. 417-431 | Heart .75 to 2.25 in. Set/3. 417-434 |

| Star .625 to 2.1 in. Set/3. 417-433 | Flower .625 to 2.1 in. Set/3. 417-435 | Leaf 1 to 3 in. Set/3. 417-437 | Funny Flower .75 to 2.3 in. Set/3. 417-436 |

Daisy
Durable plastic.
.75 to 2.5 in.
Set/3.
417-439

Wilto[n]

Candy Eyeballs
Clever icing decorations will open your eyes to so many fun decorating possibilities! Icing decorations measure $5/16$ in. diameter and are perfect additions to faces on pops, cookies, cupcakes and more. 56 pc.
1006-8024

Pops Fun Pix
Just insert these pre-made paper decorations into your pops for instant, party-ready treats.

Jungle Pals
8—2.75 x 2.5 in.
2113-1122

Princess
8—2.5 x 3 in.
2113-1106

Make-A-Face Icing Decorations
Put a face on pops, cookies, cupcakes and more. Makes 9 faces. Cetified Kosher.

People 710-1005

Animals 710-1004

Foil Wraps
For a fancy presentation, wrap pops in beautiful, bright foil squares! 12—6 x 6 in.

Jewel Tone 2113-1119

Silver 2113-1117

Ruffle Pops Wraps
Paper petals create a floral fantasy. Insert stick through hole in wrap. 8 sets, 4 in. dia.
2113-1102

Hearts and Stars Pops Wraps
Hearts and stars designs create pops excitement. Insert stick through hole in wrap. 8 sets, 4.25 and 3.5 in. diameter.
2113-0995

Hearts Pops Wraps
Say I love you with a heart-surrounded pop. Insert stick through hole in wrap. 8 sets, 4.25 and 3.5 in. diameter.
2113-1100

Pops Doilies
Fancy doily bases present pops with a touch of sophistication. Insert stick through hole in doily. 24 doilies 3.25 in. diameter.
1904-1001

Foil Candy Cups
Crisply-pleated, just like professionals use. Wax-laminated paper on foil. Pk./75.

Red 415-314
Blue 415-313
Pink 415-315
Gold 415-306
Silver 415-307

---

pops presentation
Give it your all when you present pops as gifts! Use your creativity and decorate these fun presentation pieces to match your celebration. Pops and decorations not included.

Pops Flower Pot Kit
2 containers 6 x 5.25 in.; 2 bags 7.5 in. x 2 ft; 2 ribbons 1.5 ft; 2 tags 2 in. dia.
415-1503

Pops Gift Boxes
2 boxes 8 x 6.25 x 6.25; 2 clear seals 1 in. dia.
415-1502

Pops Display Stand
Decorate it to match your celebration theme. Holds 28 pops. 12 in. dia. x 9.5 in. high; 2 border strips 1.25 in. w.; 10 and 12 in. dia.
1512-138

Pops Treat Sticks
6 plastic sticks measure 8 in. long. Insert pop or treat onto stick end with platform.
2103-1122

Pops Favor Bags
12 bags 4.25 x 7 in.; 12 ribbons 12 in.
1912-1341

Popcorn Treat Boxes
Classic shape stands up tall to hold cookies and other snacks. 3.75 x 2.25 x 5.25 in. high. White. Pk./4
1904-1141

Keeping in Touch with Wilton

There's always something new at Wilton! Fun decorating classes that will help your decorating skills soar. Exciting cake designs to challenge you. Great new decorating products to try. Helpful hints to make your decorating more efficient and successful. Here's how you can keep up to date with what's happening at Wilton.

Decorating Classes

Do you want to learn more about cake decorating, with the personal guidance of a Wilton Instructor? Wilton has two ways to help you.

The Wilton School of Cake Decorating and Confectionery Art is the home of the world's most popular cake decorating curriculum. For more than 80 years, thousands of students from around the world have learned to decorate cakes using The Wilton Method. In 1929, Dewey McKinley Wilton taught the first small classes in his Chicago home. Today, The Wilton School teaches more people to decorate than any school in the world. As the school has grown, some techniques have been refined and there are more classes to choose from— but the main philosophies of the Wilton Method have remained.

The Wilton School occupies a state-of-the-art facility in Darien, Illinois. More than 120 courses are offered each year, including The Master Course, a 2-week class that provides individualized instruction in everything from borders to flowers to constructing a tiered wedding cake. Other courses focus on specific subjects, such as the Lambeth Method, Fondant Art and Tiered Cakes. Courses in Gum Paste and Chocolate Artistry feature personal instruction from well-known experts.

For more information or to enroll, write to:
Wilton School of Cake Decorating and Confectionery Art
2240 West 75th Street, Woodridge, IL 60517
Attn: School Coordinator
Or visit: www.school.wilton.com
Or call: 800-772-7111, ext. 2888, for a free brochure and schedule.

Wilton Method Cake Decorating Classes are the convenient way to learn to decorate, close to your home. Wilton Method Classes are easy and fun for everyone. You can learn the fundamentals of cake decorating with a Wilton trained teacher in just four 2-hour sessions. When the course is over, you'll know how to decorate star and shell birthday cakes or floral anniversary cakes like a pro. Everyone has a good time—it's a great place for new decorators to discover their talent. Since 1974, more than 4 million people have enjoyed these classes. Special Project Classes also are available in subjects like candy-making, cupcakes and brownies, tall cakes, gingerbread, cookie blossoms and more.

Find classes near you!
In U.S.A., call 800-942-8881 or visit www.wilton.com
In Canada, call 416-679-0790, ext. 200, or email classprograms@wilton.ca
In Mexico, visit www.wiltonenespañol.com

Wilton Products

Visit a Wilton retailer near you. Your local Wilton retailer is the best place to see the great variety of cake decorating products made by Wilton. If you are new to decorating, it's a good idea to see these products in person; if you are an experienced decorator, you'll want to visit your Wilton retailer regularly to have the supplies you need on hand. From bakeware and icing supplies to candles and publications, most Wilton retailers carry a good stock of items needed for decorating. Remember, the selection of products changes with each season, so if you want to decorate cakes in time for upcoming holidays, visit often to stock up on current pans, colors and toppers.

Order on-line, by phone or by mail. You can also place orders 24 hours a day at our website, www.wilton.com. Shopping on-line is fast, easy and secure. Or, you can place an order by phone at 800-794-5866 (7WILTON) or by mail, using the Order Form in the Wilton Yearbook of Cake Decorating.

Wilton On The Web

www.wilton.com is the place to find Wilton decorating information on-line. It's filled with great decorating ideas and delicious recipes, updated regularly for the season. You'll also find helpful hints, answers to common decorating questions and easy shopping for great Wilton products.

Wilton Publications

We never run out of decorating ideas! Each year, Wilton publishes more new idea books based on Wilton Method techniques. When you're planning a specific occasion, Wilton books are a fantastic source of decorating inspiration.

The Wilton Yearbook of Cake Decorating is our annual showcase of the latest ideas in decorating. Each edition is packed with all-new cake ideas, instructions and products—it's the best place to find out what's new at Wilton. Cakes for every occasion throughout the year are included: holidays, graduations, birthdays, weddings and more. If you are looking for a new cake to test your decorating skills, you can't beat the Yearbook.

Wilton also regularly publishes special interest decorating books, including books on wedding and holiday decorating, candy-making, home entertaining and food gifting. Look for them wherever Wilton products are sold.